THE PLANTPOWER WAY: ITALIA

THE PLANTPOWER WAY: ITALIA

DELICIOUS VEGAN RECIPES FROM THE ITALIAN COUNTRYSIDE

JULIE PIATT + RICH ROLL

AVERY
AN IMPRINT OF PENGUIN RANDOM HOUSE
NEW YORK

AVERY

an imprint of Penguin Random House LLC
375 Hudson Street
New York, New York 10014

Copyright © 2018 by Rich Roll Enterprises LLC
Photographs courtesy of Maclay Heriot and Leia Marasovich
Decorative symbol art © Shutterstock/aniana

Most Avery books are available at special quantity discounts for bulk purchase for sales
promotions, premiums, fund-raising, and educational needs. Special books or book excerpts also
can be created to fit specific needs. For details, write SpecialMarkets@penguinrandomhouse.com.

ISBN 9780735217591
ebook ISBN 9780735217607

Printed in the United States of America

10 9 8 7 6 5 4 3 2 1

Book design by Ashley Tucker and Shawn Patterson

To our international tribe who met us on retreat, bravely faced themselves, and vulnerably bared their souls in the quest to reconnect with their authentic hearts.

And to our fellow Earthlings all over this magnificent planet who have cared enough to take responsibility for living their light and making the world brighter.

We bow to you . . .

CONTENTS

INTRODUCTION

One glorious Italian morning, I set up my yoga mat in the middle of some ancient ruins on one of the highest mountains on the Amalfi coast. It was destined to be the most epic practice. The view from there was mind-blowing and the energy ancient.

Focused on my internal energy with my eyes closed, I flowed through the asanas, feeling the life force re-awaken my body with its pranic source. When I opened my eyes momentarily, I saw that a group of local villagers had come down to the park to watch me practice. Here, pausing in downward dog, I surveyed them from my inverted, upside-down view. Then, I considered my options. Either I could stop and slink out, apologizing for my trespass, or I could stay the course and commit mindfully to my practice in spite of the distraction. I chose to stay the yogi course—I closed my eyes and continued on.

Moving with one breath, one movement, I made my way through the postures, finally coming to rest in child's pose. After a few rejuvenating breaths, I rolled up to an easy seated position. Blinking my eyes, I surveyed my surroundings again and noticed that the park had cleared completely except for one single man. He was an elderly *huomo*, upward of eighty years or so. Sitting on a park bench with both hands resting on his cane, he had been patiently waiting for me to finish. I smiled at the relic beauty of his stonelike chiseled form. He was sporting just the right combination of Italian fashion with his yellow cashmere vest and plaid driving cap. Shyly, I managed a muffled attempt at a greeting in my broken Italian. "Que bella," I said, as I gazed out at arguably the most beautiful ocean view on Earth. At first, he didn't reply, but then after a poignant pause, as if to emphasize his actions, he started to rise. He creaked and wobbled himself erect, steadied himself on his cane, and shuffled over to me with steady aim. His wrinkled and weathered palm turned upward and extended toward me like an offering. Unsure of his motives and what was happening, I sheepishly placed my hand in his. He squeezed it firmly as if to say, "Pay attention," and stared into my eyes with intense connection. His smile broke open wide, revealing a toothless cave. Bowing his head in devotion to me and in that perfectly charismatic Italian way, he kissed my hand with all the feeling of *amore* that Italians are famous for. Then he turned and shuffled out of the park.

I never forgot that moment. I considered it a truly defining moment in my life—one when my course shifted and a new path began to unfold before me. Looking back, it was as though Italy was speaking to me, telling me that a love affair I'd never experienced before awaited me there. In the years since, I have indeed fallen in love with Italy: her people, her land, and her food.

For the next eight years, I brought groups to a magnificent *borgo* called Iesolana, nestled in the heart of the magical countryside of Tuscany. Iesolana sits on two hundred acres of gorgeous landscape located between Siena and Florence and is a family-owned historic villa managed by the proprietary Florentine brothers, Giovanni and Francesco Toscano. Surrounded by rolling hills and lavender fields, when you visit, you feel as if this is the only place on Earth.

Even though there wasn't a lot of structure to the retreats I led in those years, practicing yoga twice a day in the beautiful rolling hills of the Tuscan countryside catalyzed deep connection and joy. Italy is a place pregnant with life and history, and it is a wonderful place for self-discovery. I collected deep friendships during those trips, and the experience kept giving in ways that I could not have seen from the start. Giovanni and Francesco also became like my own brothers, and it felt like a family reunion of the best kind seeing them every year.

With those memories still in my heart, Rich and I saw an opportunity to return to hosting retreats, but this time we'd marry them with our work around sustainability and food. We decided to offer plant-based retreats devoted to sharing our passion for health and wellness in exotic places in the world. Our mission is not only to transform and inspire those who wish to join us on the journey but to learn from the region we visit and make an impact too. Culinary collaboration and exchange is our goal, and our hope is to leave each place we go with a new way to approach food.

We knew without a doubt where our first stop would be: Iesolana, our home away from home, in glorious Tuscany.

Italy is celebrated for having some of the most delicious food on the planet. While many people associate Italian cooking with rich meats and dairy cheeses, dishes with fresh vegetables, legumes, fruits, nuts, and grains are just as prevalent. Italian cuisine has all of the ingredients nature intended for whole-food, plant-based cooking. And what's more, you can have extraordinary plant-based Italian cheese too. Like *This Cheese Is Nuts!*, this cookbook has recipes for creamy, crave-able, tangy, nut-based cheeses that will blow your mind and delight your taste buds. These cheeses are the secret to reinventing traditional Italian favorites so that they are healthier and sustainable but also just as delicious. Pizza Margherita? It's here (see page 98). Classic Eggplant Parmesan too (see page 230). I've also included new favorites that will excite any lover of Italian food, as well as rich and creamy gelatos for dessert.

This cookbook is a celebration of vegan Italian cooking and a way of eating that is better for your health, our environment, and our animals. You won't have to give up anything; instead, you will gain a whole new way to thrive on this beautiful planet. It's also a celebration of collaboration and the endless possibilities that come with exchanging ideas and cooking techniques across cultures.

When we first started planning the trip to Iesolana, I wondered how I would get the non-vegan resident chefs to agree to collaborate with me in this crazy adventure. A few months before we arrived, I sent the chefs, Francesca and Manuela, a copy of *The Plantpower Way* so they could start to get an idea of my recipes and process. Then I worked out the new menu and sent over recipes. Our recipes inspired them—they immediately started creating vegan dishes and showcasing classic Italian recipes like Sicilian Orange Cheese (page 76) that are already vegan. They began to engage with food in a whole new way.

During that first retreat, Francesca, Manuela, and the entire kitchen staff were like rock stars to us. Never before had the chefs cooked for a group who cared so much about the food they were eating. They felt our deep appreciation and respect for the love and care they put into preparing the food. We brought them out of the kitchen every night to honor them and to express the gratitude we had for their food. The love we shared made the experience even more special, and many of the dishes in this cookbook came out of the discoveries we made together.

Rich and I love the experience of a retreat. It's one of the most potent ways to catalyze transformation. Eating high-vibrational foods, practicing meditation and yoga, and sharing community with like-minded people provides the sustenance, clarity, and safety for us to connect to our deepest desires, discover our truest essence, and reconnect with the things we loved as children. There is something immensely powerful about leaving one's familiar environment and mundane life routines that opens a doorway for rebirth and a new life trajectory. The experience folds into our energy blueprint—it will never leave us. We hope to capture some of that magic in these pages.

As empathic humans, we all want to live harmoniously in our own bodies and with our environment and animals. We just sometimes lose our way. Living a "plantpowered" life is a journey of discovering our authentic selves and learning to connect with one another, our community, and our planet. By living the lifestyle, we all contribute to the movement. If we can cultivate the same principles in our everyday lives, we can join together to form a powerful connection and align our energies.

On the final day of our retreats, we gather in a counsel circle and vow to uphold every member of our group in their highest essence despite any appearance to the contrary. That means we've got their back. We promise to see them as their most authentic selves no matter where they are in the journey because all human beings are divine. There is nothing more beautiful or powerful than humans who know themselves. In this state of awareness, we spontaneously and naturally do good and share love.

With this book, we include you in our tribe and in this prayer.

In love and service,
Julie & Rich

**Coconut Yogurt,
Red Grapes, and
Balsamic Drizzle**
page 28

1

BLENDS AND BREAKFAST

TUSCAN CANTALOUPE-BASIL BLEND

SERVES 2 There is something very special about basil blended with Tuscan cantaloupe. I discovered this one by accident when I was out of my predictable bananas and berries. It's refreshing and uplifting. You can substitute kale for the spinach if you like.

INGREDIENTI

2 cups cantaloupe	½ orange, peeled
1 cup fresh spinach	2 cups coconut water
5 fresh basil leaves	1 tablespoon coconut oil

PREPARAZIONE

In the bowl of a Vitamix or high-speed blender, place all the ingredients and blend on medium speed for about 45 seconds, or until smooth.

FOREST MENTA BLEND

SERVES 2 A new twist on a minty, refreshing blend that is reminiscent of the woodlands. I love that all the ingredients for this blend are whole foods free of powders and processed sweeteners. If you use three dates, the color will be a deep forest green. If you opt for the sweetness of four dates, it will be a gorgeous bark color.

INGREDIENTI

2 frozen bananas

2 cups coconut milk

1½ cups fresh packed mint leaves, plus 1 mint leaf for garnish

¼ avocado

3 or 4 dates, pitted

1 tablespoon cacao nibs, for garnish

PREPARAZIONE

In the bowl of a Vitamix or high-speed blender, place the bananas, coconut milk, 1½ cups of mint leaves, avocado, and dates and blend on medium speed for 1 minute. Garnish with the cacao nibs and mint leaf. Enjoy!

MAKE SPACE FOR PEACE AND A DEEPER CONNECTION WITH YOUR GREATER SELF

How can we experience peace and true connection in our own lives as well as collectively on this planet if we don't make space for it? If you met someone you were interested in dating and you told them that you just don't have time to see them, what do you think the likely potential for that relationship would be? Obviously not that great. Yet many of us in the modern Western world spend our lives running toward some goal, object, or dream, and in that process, we also run away from ourselves and our deepest knowing of who we are. Without prioritizing moments of pause and reflection, we cannot experience the deeper awareness of what it means to be living in this moment when we connect with expanded states of being instead of doing.

Starting your day off with three bowls of puer tea creates space for the divine to find its way into your life. It's a simple ceremony that is free of dogma or ideology, which makes this practice widely accessible to all of us. We drink living tea made of tea leaves from trees that are hundreds of years old. The trees are masters of community, sharing, and exchanging with each other through the roots beneath and within the soil. They don't discriminate. They freely share with diverse species of trees. This greater awareness of community, sisterhood, and brotherhood is something we can all benefit from. We are all intricately connected whether we are aware of it or not. And as Zen tea master Wu De teaches, it's even deeper than that. He shares that we, in fact, are the very plants of this Earth. Within us are the planets, stars, sunlight, soil, and plants that grow on Earth. Drinking puer tea mindfully each day deepens our connection to nature and the Self. This presence in turn blesses everything and everyone around us. Together, we can make space for world peace to blossom.

ALMOND MILK

MAKES 4 CUPS This delicious nut milk is so incredibly simple that you will want to make it yourself. Adding some fresh vanilla bean and a pitted date produces a sweet, aromatic flavor. A generous pinch of salt helps it last a bit longer in the fridge.

INGREDIENTI

2 cups almonds   Generous pinch of salt

4 cups filtered water

———

IN ANTICIPO:

Place the almonds in filtered water in a small bowl.

Cover and refrigerate overnight.

———

1   Drain the almonds and place them in the bowl of a Vitamix or high-speed blender with the 4 cups filtered water. Add the salt. Blend on high speed for 1 minute.

2   Pour the mixture into a nut-milk bag and strain into a bowl (you can compost the pulp or freeze it to use in baked recipes).

DRIED STRAWBERRY SLICES

MAKES 1 CUP Ripe fruit that has been dehydrated can add an extra-special touch to your recipes. I use these delicate red bursts in my Brown Rice Strawberry Risotto (page 24), but they are also gorgeous pressed into Gorgonzola Blue (page 56).

INGREDIENTI

**1 pint fresh strawberries, washed,
with stems removed, cut into 3/8-inch-thick slices**

PREPARAZIONE

1   Arrange the strawberries flat on a nonstick dehydrator sheet.

2   Dehydrate on low, about 90 degrees F, until dry, about 4 hours.

BROWN RICE STRAWBERRY RISOTTO

SERVES 4 Using brown rice in place of the Arborio rice traditionally used in risotto gives this sweet summer dish a wilder, more natural texture, which I prefer. Cashew cream adds just the right amount of richness.

INGREDIENTI

2 cups short-grain brown rice

1 tablespoon olive oil

½ cup Coconut Cashew Cream (page 58)

1 cup Dried Strawberry Slices (page 23), plus extra for garnish

1 teaspoon Celtic sea salt

Freshly cracked black pepper to taste

PREPARAZIONE

1   Prepare the brown rice according to the package directions, but add 1 extra cup of water. We want the rice to be moist and wetter than usual.

2   When the rice is done, fold in the olive oil, cashew cream, dried strawberries, salt, and pepper.

3   Transfer the mixture to a serving bowl and garnish with dried strawberries.

FLORENTINE CHIA SEED PUDDING

SERVES 1 There is nothing more nourishing for our bodies than a healthy serving of superfood pudding in the morning. Chia seeds are great for digestion. This version of a morning porridge is one of my favorites. The fresh coconut makes it subtly sweet. Try not adding any extra sweetener, and after a few mornings you may find you don't miss it at all.

INGREDIENTI

½ cup chia seeds

¼ cup almonds

¼ cup shredded coconut

1 teaspoon ground cinnamon

1 teaspoon ground cardamom

1   Preheat the oven to 350 degrees F.

2   Toast the almonds on a rimmed baking sheet
for 10 minutes.

3   In a small serving bowl, combine the chia
seeds and 1 cup of filtered water. Stir for
about 3 minutes, until the chia seeds become
gelatinous in texture. Add the coconut,
cinnamon, and cardamom to the chia seed
mixture.

4   Garnish with the toasted almonds.

COCONUT YOGURT, RED GRAPES, AND BALSAMIC DRIZZLE

SERVES 2 A yogurt you can celebrate. The coconut meat and milk give it a high, fresh vibe while the sweet red grapes infuse you with heart-healing resveratrol. Balsamic glaze adds the perfect finish.

INGREDIENTI

Coconut Yogurt:

2 cups fresh young coconut meat

1 cup coconut milk

2 capsules acidophilus (3-billion-active-culture strain)

Red Grapes:

1/2 cup sweet red grapes

Balsamic Drizzle:

1 cup balsamic vinegar

1/4 cup organic sugar

PREPARAZIONE

1 **To make the coconut yogurt:** In the bowl of a Vitamix or high-speed blender, place the coconut meat, coconut milk, and acidophilus and blend on medium speed until smooth.

2 Transfer the mixture to a mason jar (make sure to fill it only half full). Secure the lid and dehydrate in a dehydrator at 110 degrees F for at least 12 hours or overnight. Remove the lid and stir well. Transfer the mason jar with the yogurt to the refrigerator to chill, about 3 hours.

3 **To arrange the grapes:** Place some grapes in the bottom of each of two pretty glasses.

4 **To make the balsamic drizzle:** Place the vinegar and the sugar in a small saucepan over medium-low heat until the sugar dissolves and the vinegar reduces down to form a glaze, approximately 8 to 10 minutes. Remove from the heat and set aside.

5 **To assemble:** Spoon the coconut yogurt over the grapes and drizzle with 2 tablespoons of the balsamic mixture.

MORNING POLENTA PORRIDGE

SERVES 2 Eating a bowl of warm porridge in the morning is a great way to balance our adrenals. Porridge is also a delicious and hearty alternative to oatmeal. Make certain the polenta you use is organic and try leaving out the maple syrup or any other sweeteners. After your taste buds adjust, you will notice that the sweetness of the banana or other fruit is enhanced.

INGREDIENTI

1 cup polenta	Maple syrup (optional)
¼ cup chia seeds	Pinch of ground nutmeg
1 banana or ½ cup ripe fruit	

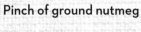

PREPARAZIONE

1   In a small saucepan, bring 3 cups of water to a boil and add the polenta. Reduce the heat to low, cover the saucepan with a lid, and simmer for about 8 minutes, until the polenta is soft.

2   In a small bowl, soak the chia seeds in ½ cup filtered water and stir for about 5 minutes, until the chia seeds become gelatinous.

3   Add the chia seed mixture to the warm polenta and stir to incorporate well.

4   Transfer the mixture to serving bowls and top with sliced bananas or ripe fruit.

5   Sprinkle with syrup, if desired, and nutmeg and enjoy.

MOOD FOLLOWS ACTION

Our bodies are sacred temples for our soul. We need to move our bodies to get the blood moving, the muscles strengthened, and the toxins—both physical and emotional—releasing. We are living longer than ever, and it is vital that we care for our bodies. It's a guarantee that you are going to feel very different after moving your body. It doesn't matter what your choice of movement is, only that it's one you enjoy. Get outside in nature every day and become one with your breath. That is true healing for body and soul. Living a triumphant life or a life of "JAI" requires that we treat our bodies as sacred temples for our souls. Moving our bodies is synonymous with caring for our spirit. So get outside and get it done!

Almond Fennel Pesto
page 48

2
SAUCES, SPREADS, AND CHEESES

PORCINI TOMATO SAUCE

WALNUT PORCINI CREAM SAUCE

BEET TOMATO SAUCE

SUN-DRIED TOMATO SAUCE

MATHIS'S SIMPLY RED TOMATO SAUCE

BLACK PESTO

CHEESY PESTO

ALMOND FENNEL PESTO

OLIVE AND SUN-DRIED TOMATO TAPENADE

ROASTED PINE NUT (PIGNOLI) SPREAD

OLIVE WALNUT SPREAD

ROASTED ALMOND SUN-DRIED TOMATO CHEESE

CREAMY GARLIC GORGONZOLA

COCONUT CASHEW CREAM

CLASSIC CASHEW CHEESE SAUCE

MACADAMIA CASHEW BURRATA

CASHEW ALMOND MOZZARELLA

CAPRINO (ITALIAN GOAT CHEESE)

CASHEW ALMOND RICOTTA

MACADAMIA PARMESAN

CASHEW PARMESAN

SMOKED WALNUT PARMESAN

SICILIAN ORANGE CHEESE

MOZZARELLA BALLS IN BRINE

PORCINI TOMATO SAUCE

MAKES 2 CUPS The rich, warming flavor of this sauce will make you crave it. I adore porcini mushrooms served in tomato sauce over pasta. For this sauce, I pureed the mushrooms with the tomatoes and spices in the bowl of a Vitamix. The result is heavenly. You'll want to double the recipe to allow for second helpings.

INGREDIENTI

½ cup dried porcini mushrooms

1 pint cherry tomatoes, stems removed

2 tablespoons fresh oregano

¼ cup olive oil

1 teaspoon large-grain Celtic sea salt

Freshly cracked pepper

IN ANTICIPO:

Pour 1 cup of boiling water over the mushrooms in a small bowl and let them steep for about 1 hour.

———

PREPARAZIONE

1 Heat a cast-iron skillet over high heat and add the tomatoes. Cook them only until slightly black on one side. Do not use any oil in the pan.

2 In the bowl of a Vitamix or high-speed blender, place the tomatoes, mushrooms plus the mushroom soaking liquid, oregano, olive oil, and salt. Blend on medium speed for 1 minute.

3 Transfer the mixture to a large, flat saucepan and warm over low heat. Adjust the seasonings to taste, adding more salt, pepper, and oregano as desired.

WALNUT PORCINI CREAM SAUCE

SERVES 4 TO 6 I can't really decide which ingredient in this dish puts it over the top. Each flavor is so special on its own that it's hard to miss with this combination. This sauce is full-bodied, rich, and creamy. The miso is already very salty but, depending on which pasta you use, feel free to sprinkle a bit of Celtic sea salt on the top. This sauce is also divine over mashed potatoes.

INGREDIENTI

½ cup dried porcini mushrooms

2 cups raw local walnuts

¼ cup barley miso

Freshly cracked black pepper to taste

Celtic sea salt (optional)

PREPARAZIONE

1 In the bowl of a Vitamix or high-speed blender, place the walnuts, miso, and porcini with the soaking water and blend on medium speed for 1 minute or until smooth.

2 If you want a thinner consistency for your sauce, add filtered water in increments of ¼ cup at a time, not exceeding 1 cup.

3 Pour the sauce over fresh hot pasta of your choice and toss to coat.

4 Grind fresh pepper over the top and adjust the salt as desired.

BEET TOMATO SAUCE

MAKES 3 CUPS Deep hues of nature-infused reds bloom in this delicious, hearty sauce. I adore it on my Classic Family-Style Pizza (page 94) and in Classic Eggplant Parmesan (page 230).

INGREDIENTI

6 Roma tomatoes	1 tablespoon olive oil
1 shallot, sliced	1 teaspoon Celtic sea salt
1 medium beet	2 tablespoons fresh oregano
8 sun-dried tomatoes in oil	1 tablespoon fresh fennel

PREPARAZIONE

1   Heat a cast-iron wok or deep saucepan over high heat and add the tomatoes. Cook the tomatoes until blackened (do not use oil).

2   Add the shallot slices to the tomato mixture and sauté until they are browned, about 5 minutes.

3   Bring 3 cups of water to a boil in a small saucepan and add the beet. Cook for about 40 minutes, until tender. Drain the beet and remove the skin.

4   In the bowl of a Vitamix or high-speed blender, place the Roma tomato–shallot mixture, beet, sun-dried tomatoes, olive oil, salt, oregano, and fennel. Blend on high speed for 1 minute.

SUN-DRIED TOMATO SAUCE

MAKES 2 CUPS This version of a traditional tomato sauce is a bit richer and saltier than those that use only tomatoes. I like it with my pasta—puttanesca style, adding olives and capers. A bit of seaweed gives it the slightly fishy flavor reminiscent of anchovies in Italian cuisine.

INGREDIENTI

1 pint cherry tomatoes, stems removed

One 8-ounce jar of sun-dried tomatoes in oil

½ medium carrot

1 to 2 teaspoons seaweed flakes

5 fresh basil leaves

2 tablespoons fresh oregano

Pinch of Celtic sea salt

PREPARAZIONE

1   In the bowl of a Vitamix or high-speed blender, place the tomatoes, sun-dried tomatoes with oil, carrot, seaweed, basil, oregano, and salt. Blend on medium speed for 1 minute or until smooth.

2   Transfer the sauce to a flat saucepan and warm over low heat. Adjust the seasonings to taste.

MATHIS'S SIMPLY RED TOMATO SAUCE

MAKES 3 CUPS My daughter Mathis studied plant-based Italian cooking for her seventh-grade semester project. She developed this recipe and shared it with me.

INGREDIENTI

7 garden tomatoes on the vine

3 garlic cloves, peeled and minced

1/2 cup chopped onion

2 tablespoons olive oil

1 teaspoon Celtic sea salt

1/2 teaspoon freshly cracked black pepper

PREPARAZIONE

1 In a deep saucepan, bring 6 cups of water to a boil over high heat and add the tomatoes. Boil for 5 minutes or until the skin begins to peel off.

2 In the pitcher of a Vitamix or high-speed blender, place the tomatoes, garlic, and onion. Blend on medium speed for 30 seconds. Then add water in 2-tablespoon increments and blend again to reach the desired consistency.

3 Pour the blended sauce into a saucepan over medium-low heat and add the olive oil. Heat until warm, about 5 minutes. Add the salt and pepper to taste.

BLACK PESTO

MAKES 2 1/2 CUPS This is a wonderful variation on a classic pesto. The black color comes from using fermented garlic. You can find fermented garlic in a Japanese market or at Whole Foods. It has a mild, sweet taste.

INGREDIENTI

2 cups raw pine nuts (pignoli)

2 cups packed fresh basil

1 head fermented black garlic

2 tablespoons olive oil

1/2 to 1 teaspoon Celtic sea salt

PREPARAZIONE

1   Preheat the oven to 350 degrees F.

2   Place the pine nuts on a rimmed baking sheet and roast them for 5 to 8 minutes or until golden brown.

3   In the pitcher of a Vitamix or high-speed blender, place the basil first, then the pine nuts, garlic, olive oil, and salt. Blend on low speed using the plunger to distribute the mixture evenly or until the mixture forms a paste or pesto consistency.

4   Adjust the salt to taste. Feel free to add a bit more oil or filtered water in increments of 2 tablespoons if you want a thinner pesto.

CHEESY PESTO

MAKES 2 CUPS Roasting the pine nuts is my secret to achieving an extra-cheesy taste in this pesto. It will liven up any pasta, and it is also a great filling for my Ravioli (page 194). Use it as a spread on your favorite panini. Just be sure to make an extra batch to keep on hand! You can store it in the fridge for up to a week.

INGREDIENTI

2 cups raw pine nuts (pignoli)   ½ teaspoon Celtic sea salt

2 cups packed fresh basil leaves   2 tablespoons olive oil

PREPARAZIONE

1   Preheat the oven to 350 degrees F.

2   Place the pine nuts on a rimmed baking sheet and roast them for 5 to 8 minutes or until golden brown.

3   In the bowl of a Vitamix or high-speed blender, place the basil first, then the roasted pine nuts, olive oil, and salt. Blend on low speed using the plunger to distribute the mixture evenly or until the mixture forms a paste or pesto consistency.

ALMOND FENNEL PESTO

MAKES 2½ CUPS The licorice note of fresh fennel brings a unique twist to this pesto. Fennel grows wild in the Italian countryside and is a local herb that has a calming effect on digestion.

INGREDIENTI

2 cups raw almonds

2 cups fresh basil leaves

½ cup fennel tops, chopped

2 teaspoons Celtic sea salt

¼ cup olive oil

Juice of ½ lemon

½ avocado

———

IN ANTICIPO:

**Place the almonds in filtered water in a small bowl.
Cover and refrigerate overnight.**

———

PREPARAZIONE

1   Drain the almonds.

2   In the bowl of a food processor, place the
    basil leaves first, then the fennel tops, drained
    almonds, salt, olive oil, lemon juice, and
    avocado.

3   Pulse until the mixture is well incorporated
    and mealy in texture. You can adjust the
    consistency by adding small increments of
    water, 2 tablespoons at a time.

4   Store this pesto in a glass container for up to
    1 week.

OLIVE AND SUN-DRIED TOMATO TAPENADE

MAKES 2 CUPS Convenient by design, this simple tapenade could qualify as fast food. It uses only three ingredients. The salt and seasonings in the prepared sun-dried tomatoes and olives are sufficient for lively flavor in this recipe.

INGREDIENTI

1 Roma tomato or
1 medium garden-variety tomato

One 8-ounce jar of
sun-dried tomatoes in oil

16 kalamata olives

PREPARAZIONE

1   In the bowl of a food processor, place all the ingredients and pulse until they combine to a spreadable consistency.

2   Serve as a dip or spread.

ROASTED PINE NUT (PIGNOLI) SPREAD

SERVES 6 I love this nut cheese—it's so incredibly simple yet bursting with flavor. The secret to the irresistible taste is the roasting of the pine nuts, which brings it to a whole new level of "yum."

INGREDIENTI

2 cups pine nuts (pignoli)   1 teaspoon Celtic sea salt
2 tablespoons olive oil

PREPARAZIONE

1   Preheat the oven to 350 degrees F.

2   Arrange the pine nuts in a single layer on a rimmed baking sheet and roast them for about 8 minutes or until they turn golden brown.

3   In the bowl of a food processor, place the pine nuts and pulse until they are mealy in texture.

4   With the motor running, pour in the olive oil and add the salt.

5   Use as a spread, a dip, or a filling.

OLIVE WALNUT SPREAD

MAKES 2 CUPS This condiment is perfect on any panini (or what we now call "toasties"). Walnuts are the only nuts you don't need to soak. They are a miraculous brain food.

INGREDIENTI

2 cups packed fresh spinach

2 cups walnuts

One 5.6-ounce jar of kalamata olives or 1½ cups kalamata olives, drained

1 garlic clove, peeled

PREPARAZIONE

1 In the bowl of a food processor, place the spinach first, then the walnuts, olives, and garlic.

2 Pulse until they are mealy in texture. Be careful not to overdo it (I prefer a rustic texture).

3 Spread on fermented sourdough or rustic country bread.

ROASTED ALMOND SUN-DRIED TOMATO CHEESE

MAKES 2½ CUPS Roasted almonds give this cheese an enhanced nutty flavor. I love to serve it as an appetizer along with fresh fruit and gluten-free crackers or slices of fermented sourdough bread. This Italian twist on almond cheese never sticks around very long in my kitchen. I've learned to make a triple batch if I want my guests to enjoy a serving!

INGREDIENTI

2 cups raw almonds

1 cup sun-dried tomatoes in oil

4 tablespoons nutritional yeast

1 tablespoon fresh oregano

4 tablespoons olive oil

1 teaspoon Celtic sea salt

PREPARAZIONE

1   Preheat the oven to 350 degrees F. Place the almonds on a rimmed baking sheet and roast them for about 8 minutes, until dark brown.

2   In the bowl of a food processor, place the sun-dried tomatoes, roasted almonds, nutritional yeast, oregano, olive oil, and salt. Process until smooth. Adjust the salt.

CREAMY GARLIC GORGONZOLA

MAKES ONE 4-INCH ROUND This is a variation on a recipe from my book *This Cheese Is Nuts!* It's so rich and creamy, you will not believe it's dairy-free. You can experiment with this cheese by adjusting the quantities of nutritional yeast or try leaving out the garlic altogether. Make sure you wash the Irish moss well or your cheese will have hints of the sea. You can marble in spirulina if you want Gorgonzola Blue.

INGREDIENTI

2 cups cashews

2 tablespoons Irish moss

1 capsule acidophilus
(3-billion-active-culture strain)

2 teaspoons coconut oil

4 tablespoons nutritional yeast

1½ teaspoons Celtic sea salt

1 small garlic clove

¼ cup filtered water

¼ to ½ teaspoon spirulina
(optional; for Gorgonzola Blue)

IN ANTICIPO:
Place the cashews in filtered water in a small bowl.
Cover and refrigerate overnight.

PREPARAZIONE

1   Rinse the Irish moss well in a colander until all the sand is removed and the smell of the ocean is gone. Oil a 4-inch mini springform pan with 1/2 teaspoon coconut oil.

2   In the pitcher of a Vitamix or high-speed blender, place 1/4 cup Irish moss and 1/2 cup of water. Blend on high speed for 1 minute or until emulsified. Pour into a small bowl and set aside. Rinse the Vitamix pitcher well, making sure the smell of Irish moss has been washed away. Drain the cashews into a colander.

3   In the clean pitcher of the Vitamix, add 2 tablespoons of the emulsified Irish moss. (Store the remainder in a mason jar refrigerated for up to 2 weeks.) Add the cashews, acidophilus, nutritional yeast, salt, garlic, the remaining 1 1/2 teaspoons coconut oil, and 1/4 cup filtered water into the pitcher of the Vitamix. Blend on medium speed until well incorporated, using the plunger to distribute the mixture well.

4   Fold the mixture into the prepared pan. Smooth out the top with a rubber spatula. If making Gorgonzola Blue, add the spirulina and fold in to marble the mixture. Do not overmix or your cheese will turn green. Cover the pan with parchment paper. Place the pan in the dehydrator and dehydrate at 90 degrees F for 24 hours. Transfer the cheese to the refrigerator for 24 hours.

5   Remove the cheese from the pan. Scrape bits from the sides and bottom of the pan and reincorporate them into the cheese, forming and smoothing it with a butter knife.

6   Serve now as a softer, creamier spread or as a pasta sauce, or place it in a wine cooler or humidifier for up to 3 weeks. Turn the cheese every few days and sprinkle it with fine salt to prevent black mold. If mold appears, cut it off and discard.

COCONUT CASHEW CREAM

MAKES ABOUT 3 CUPS This cream is heavenly. I use it in my Brown Rice Strawberry Risotto (page 24), and it is a beautiful contrast to the warm berries in my Blackberry Trifle with Coconut Cashew Cream (page 312). Try leaving the agave out entirely for a subtler dessert experience.

INGREDIENTI

2 cups cashews

2 cups fresh grated coconut

1 cup aquafaba (liquid from canned garbanzo beans)

¼ cup agave

IN ANTICIPO:

Place the cashews in filtered water in a small bowl. Cover and refrigerate overnight.

PREPARAZIONE

1 Drain the cashews. In the bowl of a food processor, place the drained cashews and coconut and pulse until they are well incorporated. With the motor running, add the aquafaba and process for about 2 minutes, until smooth.

2 Transfer the mixture to the bowl of a Vitamix or high-speed blender and add the agave. Process again for 2 more minutes to reach your desired smoothness.

CLASSIC CASHEW CHEESE SAUCE

MAKES 2 CUPS Try it with Classic Family-Style Pizza (page 94) and Classic Eggplant Parmesan (page 230), and enjoy!

INGREDIENTI

2 cups cashews

2 tablespoons chickpea miso paste

1 tablespoon coconut oil

1/4 cup nutritional yeast

1 teaspoon fresh lemon juice

1/2 teaspoon Celtic sea salt

1 cup boiling water, plus more as needed

IN ANTICIPO:

Place the cashews in filtered water in a small bowl. Cover and refrigerate overnight.

PREPARAZIONE

Drain the cashews. In the bowl of a Vitamix, blend together all the ingredients over medium speed, using the plunger to evenly distribute the mixture. Add the hot water, 1/4 cup at a time, until the desired consistency is reached. Adjust the seasonings to taste.

MACADAMIA CASHEW BURRATA

MAKES ABOUT 2 CUPS Making this cheese is a gorgeous process from start to finish. I love creating this bundle of joy and hanging it in my kitchen. My mouth starts watering just knowing that tomorrow I will have a delicious, fresh cheese to enjoy in my recipes. Just make sure you hang it high and out of reach from your pets! My Great Pyrenees, Moses, snatched my bundle from the fireplace mantel and devoured this cheese early one morning. All that remained was the cheesecloth and string! This cheese is delicious in the Wild Arugula Heirloom Salad (page 258).

INGREDIENTI

1½ cups raw macadamia nuts

½ cup whole raw cashews

1 capsule acidophilus (3-billion-active-culture strain)

1 teaspoon Celtic sea salt, plus more to taste

1½ cups coconut milk

2 teaspoons coconut oil

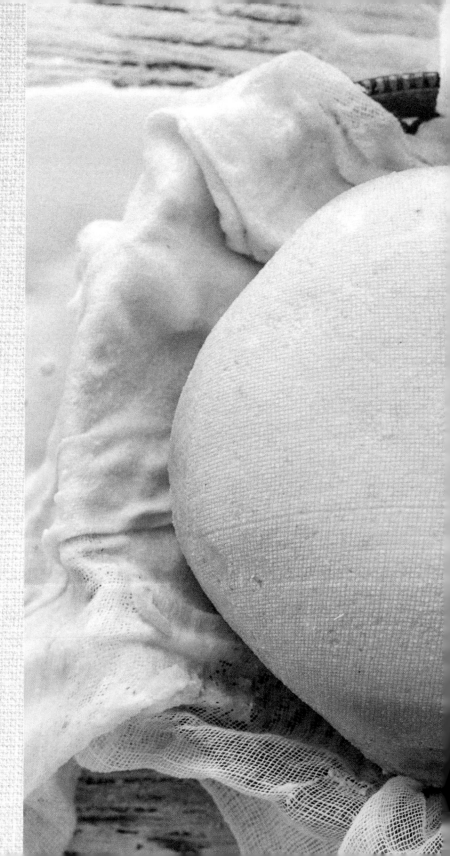

IN ANTICIPO:
Place the macadamia nuts and cashews in filtered water
in a small bowl. Cover and refrigerate overnight.

PREPARAZIONE

1   Drain the macadamia nuts and cashews.

2   In the bowl of a Vitamix or high-speed
blender, place the macadamia nuts, cashews,
acidophilus, salt, ½ cup coconut milk, and the
coconut oil and blend on medium speed until
smooth, using the plunger to evenly distribute
the mixture until well incorporated.

3   Fold the mixture into the center of an 8-inch
piece of fine cheesecloth. Gather the edges and
tie them into a bundle with string.

4   Hang the cheese bundle from a hook on the
wall, from the fireplace mantel, or under a
cupboard for 24 to 48 hours, or until a thin rind
sets up on the outside. You can place a small
dish beneath it to catch any moisture drips.

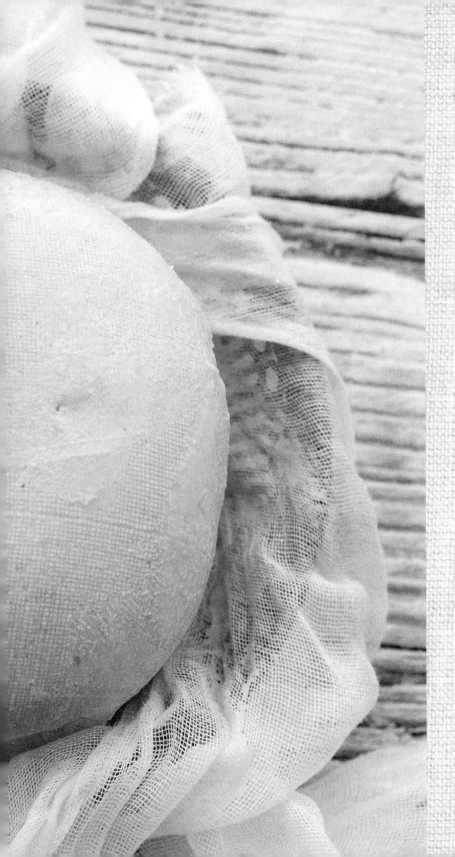

5   In a small bowl, place the remaining 1 cup of coconut milk. Add the cheese bundle to the coconut milk bath and place it in the refrigerator for 1 to 3 days.

6   Remove the cheese bundle from the refrigerator and let it sit at room temperature for an hour so the coconut milk becomes liquid. Remove the cheese bundle from the coconut milk and open it on a cutting board. Using a sharp knife, slice thin sections and lay them over a bed of arugula. Spoon a tablespoon of coconut milk over each cheese slice. If the coconut milk is still solid in places, you can use a wire whisk to smooth out the consistency.

7   Drizzle with olive oil and vinegar. Season with salt and pepper.

CASHEW ALMOND MOZZARELLA

MAKES TWO 6 X 3.5 X 2-INCH RECTANGULAR MOLDS A compassionate version of this delicious mild classic. Perfect for pizzas or panini.

INGREDIENTI

1 cup raw cashews

1 cup almonds

1 teaspoon apple cider vinegar

1 teaspoon Celtic sea salt

One 15-ounce can of coconut milk

¼ cup refined coconut oil

½ cup agar-agar flakes

IN ANTICIPO:

1. Place the cashews in filtered water in a small bowl.
Cover and refrigerate overnight.
2. Rinse the almonds well. Place them in water in a small bowl.
Cover and refrigerate overnight.

PREPARAZIONE

1. Line two 6-inch rectangular nonstick molds with plastic wrap, leaving enough hanging over the sides to wrap the mixture once it's cooled.

2. Bring 4 cups of water to a boil in medium saucepan over medium-high heat. Add the almonds and blanch them for 1 minute. Drain the almonds in a colander and remove the skins with your fingers (you can compost the skins). Drain the cashews. In the bowl of a food processor, place the almonds and cashews and pulse until they are mealy in texture. Add the vinegar and salt. Pulse again a few times to combine.

3. In a small saucepan over medium heat, combine the coconut milk, coconut oil, and 1 cup of filtered water. When the mixture is warmed through, add the agar-agar flakes and stir constantly until the agar-agar is dissolved.

4. With the motor running, pour the mixture into the food processor tube and blend until the mixture is creamy. Stop the motor, remove the lid, and scrape down the sides. Process the mixture again to make sure it gets incorporated well. This can also be done in a Vitamix for a smoother texture.

5. Pour the mixture into the prepared molds and let it cool on the counter. After the cheese has cooled, cover it with the excess plastic wrap and refrigerate it for 24 hours, or until firm.

6. Turn the cheese out of the molds and slice.

7. Use as a topping for Buffalo Cauliflower, Pineapple and Porcini Bacon Pizza (page 106), or inside a tomato-basil panini.

CAPRINO (ITALIAN GOAT CHEESE)

MAKES ABOUT 2 CUPS Fresh and similar in texture to a classic goat cheese, I created this plant-based version as a love offering to the goats of Italy. Aromatic herbs and peppercorns deliver regional flavors that perfectly complement this cheese.

INGREDIENTI

1 cup raw cashews

1 cup raw macadamia nuts

1 tablespoon apple cider vinegar

1 teaspoon Celtic sea salt

½ cup aquafaba (liquid from canned garbanzo beans)

Star anise, juniper berries, and poppy seeds

IN ANTICIPO:

Place the cashews in filtered water in a small bowl.
Cover and refrigerate overnight.

PREPARAZIONE

1 Drain the cashews.

2 In the bowl of a Vitamix or high-speed blender, place the cashews, macadamia nuts, vinegar, salt, and aquafaba. Blend on medium speed, using the plunger to evenly distribute the mixture until well incorporated.

3 Transfer the mixture to the center of an 8-inch piece of fine cheesecloth. Gather the edges and tie them into a bundle with string. Place the cheesecloth bundle in a dehydrator and dehydrate at 90 to 100 degrees F for 24 hours.

4 Divide the cheese into two equal parts. Transfer one part to a 10-inch piece of parchment paper. Using the parchment paper, roll the cheese back and forth inside to form a roll. Repeat with the other half of the mixture.

5 Refrigerate in the parchment paper overnight. Remove the parchment and garnish with star anise, juniper berries, and poppy seeds.

CASHEW
ALMOND
RICOTTA

MAKES ABOUT 2 CUPS This recipe achieves a ricotta nut cheese without any complicated aging. It is divine inside my Family Potato and Carrot Lasagna (page 164). I like to use a combination of cashews and almonds for this recipe, but if you don't have one or the other, you can use all cashews or all almonds. You can use a food processor for this recipe, but the cheese will be grainier.

INGREDIENTI

1 cup raw cashews	Juice of 1 lemon
1 cup raw almonds	

———

IN ANTICIPO:
Place the cashews in filtered water in a small bowl.
Cover and refrigerate overnight.

———

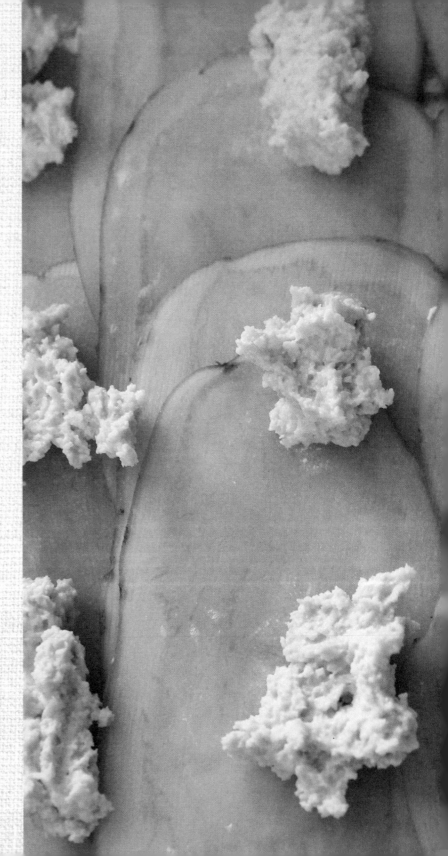

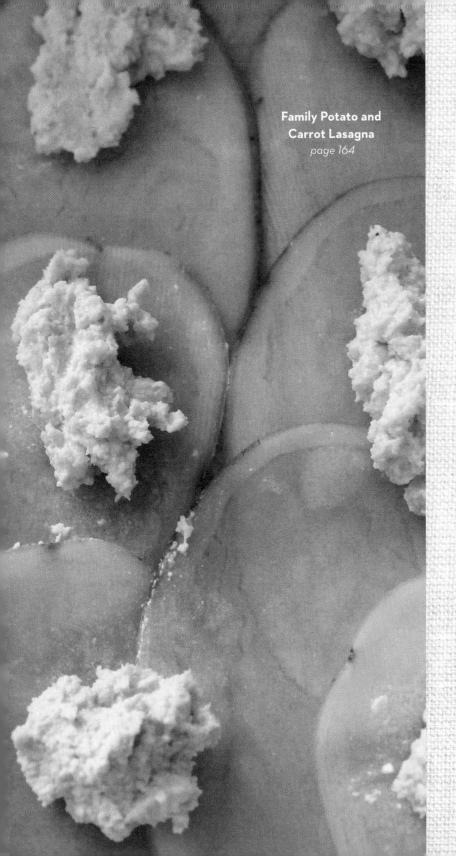

Family Potato and Carrot Lasagna
page 164

PREPARAZIONE

1   Drain the cashews.

2   **Blanch the almonds:** Bring water to a boil in a small saucepan over high heat and add the almonds. Boil for 1 minute. Remove from the heat and drain in a colander. The skins should easily rub off with your fingers.

3   In the pitcher of a Vitamix or a high-speed blender, place the cashews, blanched almonds, and lemon juice. Blend on medium speed, using the plunger to evenly redistribute the mixture until you achieve a curdlike consistency. Don't be shy—really get in there and work the plunger on all sides of the bowl. If the mixture is a bit dry, you can add 2 tablespoons of filtered water.

4   Transfer the mixture to the center of an 8-inch piece of cheesecloth. Gather the edges and tie them into a bundle with string.

5   Refrigerate the cheese bundle for 24 hours or overnight.

MACADAMIA PARMESAN

MAKES ABOUT 2 CUPS One of my great culinary achievements in plant-based cheese. It's mind-blowing how similar this cheese tastes to traditional Parmigiano-Reggiano. This recipe is versatile and can be used as a topping on many of the savory recipes in this book.

INGREDIENTI

2 cups raw macadamia nuts

1 tablespoon chickpea miso paste or light yellow miso

2 tablespoons nutritional yeast

1 teaspoon Celtic sea salt

1 capsule acidophilus (3-billion-active-culture strain)

1 tablespoon refined coconut oil, plus more for greasing the mold

PREPARAZIONE

1   Place the macadamia nuts in the bowl of a food
    processor and pulse until mealy.

2   Add the miso and pulse for 15 seconds.

3   Add the nutritional yeast, salt, and acidophilus
    and pulse for 15 seconds.

4   Add the coconut oil and process.

5   Grease a 6 x 3½ x 2-inch rectangular mold with
    coconut oil or line with plastic wrap.

6   Press the mixture firmly into the mold, cover
    with parchment paper, and refrigerate for
    24 to 48 hours.

7   Turn the cheese out of the mold and place it
    on a cutting board. Cut with a very sharp knife
    or crumble. This cheese will keep for about
    2 weeks covered and refrigerated.

CASHEW PARMESAN

MAKES ABOUT 1 CUP Making vegan Parmesan is so easy in this recipe—you just need four ingredients. If you skip soaking the nuts, your cheese will have a firmer texture. It's brilliant and useful, as one can prepare it just as the pasta water is boiling.

INGREDIENTI

1 cup cashews
(can be soaked overnight or not)

2 tablespoons miso paste

1 large garlic clove

¼ cup nutritional yeast

PREPARAZIONE

1   In the bowl of a food processor, place the cashews, miso, garlic, and nutritional yeast. Pulse until mealy in texture.

2   Store in a glass storage container. It will keep for up to 1 week refrigerated.

SMOKED WALNUT PARMESAN

MAKES ABOUT 1 CUP Brain food in a cheese, with a smoky twist.

INGREDIENTI

1 cup walnuts

2 tablespoons miso paste

1 garlic clove

4 tablespoons nutritional yeast

1 teaspoon smoked salt

PREPARAZIONE

1   In the bowl of a food processor, place the walnuts, miso, garlic, nutritional yeast, and salt. Pulse until mealy in texture.

2   Store in a glass container. It will keep for up to 1 week refrigerated.

SICILIAN ORANGE CHEESE

MAKES ONE 6-INCH HALF MOON The chefs at Iesolana were excited to show me how to make this ancient vegan *fromaggio* that hails from Sicily. It is oven baked at a very low temperature, which forms a beautiful golden rind.

INGREDIENTI

2 cups raw almonds	1½ teaspoons Celtic sea salt
1 tablespoon nutritional yeast	1 teaspoon coconut oil
1 tablespoon orange zest	¼ to ½ cup filtered water

IN ANTICIPO:

Blanch the almonds: Bring water to a boil in a small saucepan over high heat and add the almonds. Boil for 1 minute. Remove the almonds from the heat and drain them in a colander. The skins should easily rub off with your fingers. Place the skinned almonds in filtered water in a small bowl. Cover and refrigerate overnight.

PREPARAZIONE

1 Drain the almonds.

2 In the bowl of a Vitamix or high-speed blender, place the almonds, nutritional yeast, orange zest, salt, and ¼ cup of filtered water. Blend on medium speed, using the plunger to evenly distribute the mixture until well incorporated. If the mixture is too dry, add another ¼ water and incorporate again.

3 Transfer the mixture to a sieve resting over a bowl, cover with parchment paper, and place in the refrigerator for 24 hours, allowing any moisture to drain.

4 Preheat the oven to 325 degrees F. Grease a flat baking sheet with the coconut oil. Line a small bowl with plastic wrap. Turn the cheese out into the bowl and press firmly and evenly. Turn the bowl upside down over the prepared baking sheet. Remove the plastic.

5 Bake for 1 hour, or until golden on the outside.

MOZZARELLA BALLS IN BRINE

MAKES TWELVE 1-INCH MOZZARELLA BALLS One of the star recipes from *This Cheese Is Nuts!*, I am thrilled to include this cheese in this Italian collection of delicious, soft, creamy plant-based cheeses!

INGREDIENTI

Brine:	Cheese:
4 tablespoons Celtic sea salt	1 cup raw cashews
	1 cup raw almonds
	¼ cup modified tapioca starch
	¼ cup refined coconut oil
	1 teaspoon Celtic sea salt
	2½ tablespoons agar-agar flakes or 1½ teaspoons agar-agar powder
	1 cup filtered water

IN ANTICIPO:

1. Place the cashews in filtered water in a small bowl. Cover and refrigerate overnight.
2. Rinse the almonds well. Place them in filtered water in a small bowl. Cover and refrigerate overnight.

PREPARAZIONE

1   Prepare a brine solution by bringing 1 cup of filtered water to a boil in a small saucepan over high heat and adding 4 tablespoons salt until it dissolves. In a large glass bowl or mason jar add the remaining 11 cups of water. Now add the brine solution and stir to incorporate. Add 2 cups of ice. Place the brine in the refrigerator.

2   Bring 4 cups of water to a boil in a medium saucepan over medium-high heat. Add the almonds and blanch them for 1 minute. Drain the almonds in a colander and remove the skins with your fingers (you can compost the skins).

3   Drain the cashews. In the bowl of a Vitamix, place the cashews, almonds, 1 cup of filtered water, tapioca starch, coconut oil, 1 teaspoon salt, and agar-agar. Blend on high speed for 1 minute or until smooth.

4   Transfer the mixture to a small saucepan and heat over medium-low heat. Using a rubber spatula stir continuously until it becomes thick and cheese-like in consistency. (You can use a thermometer and heat the mixture to about 145 degrees F.) If the mixture becomes lumpy, remove it from the flame and whisk until smooth then return it to the heat and continue stirring.

5   Scoop the warm cheese from the saucepan with an ice-cream scooper (with a release mechanism) and drop it directly into the brine.

6   Add more ice to the cheese-brine mixture. Cover and refrigerate overnight.

WHOLE BODY BREATHING

"Whole Body Breathing" is a moving meditation, activating the life force in your body with "being-ness." Practicing yoga brings the body, heart, and spirit into divine alignment. It taps you into the greater life force and directly connects you with your heart's deepest desires. Profoundly transformational, an asana and meditation practice will carry you through every experience of life. Once you connect with this ancient wellness practice, you will never leave it. Yoga is a sacred shelter from the storm, and also the wind in your sails, allowing a miraculous divine grace to carry you. As you feel your whole body breathing, you will come to experience that you are the ultimate self-sustainable ecosystem. The Ultimate Green is You.

Classic Family-Style Pizza
page 94

3

PIZZAS

STARTER
FOR DOUGH
(SPELT, OAT, OO, ETC.)

MAKES ABOUT 1 CUP Making your own starter is so easy, and it's a healthier way to make breads and pizza crust than using packaged yeast. You can use any flour. Just make sure you feed your starter with its own kind. For example, feed spelt with spelt, OO with OO, oat with oat, and so on. Once you get the hang of it, your mind will be free to create amazing dough. The ratio of flour to water is 1:1. Credit for this recipe and the Spelt Pizza Dough (page 88) goes to Stephen and David from the Happy Pear in Ireland.

INGREDIENTI

½ cup spelt flour   ½ cup filtered water

PREPARAZIONE

1 In a mason jar, place the flour and filtered water. Stir well and set aside
   for 8 to 24 hours.

2 Feed your starter every day by removing ¼ cup so that ¼ cup is remaining. Visit
   it each day and add in more flour and water in 1:1 increments. The consistency
   should be like that of pancake batter.

3 Use what you take out in bread or crust recipes.

SPELT PIZZA DOUGH

MAKES ONE 13-INCH OR TWO 8-INCH ROUNDS Spelt is a low-gluten flour that makes a healthy-tasting pizza crust. It works well with all the pizza recipes in this section.

INGREDIENTI

1 cup spelt flour, plus more for dusting the work surface

½ cup Starter for Dough (page 86)

2 tablespoons olive oil, plus more for brushing

1 teaspoon Celtic sea salt

PREPARAZIONE

1 Add a handful of flour to a work surface or large cutting board.

2 Turn the 1 cup of flour out on the surface and make a well in the center. Add the starter, olive oil, and salt.

3 Start to incorporate the dough using your hands and working from the outside in until a dough starts to form.

4 Knead the dough with the heels of your hands, turning it over until it becomes smooth to the touch.

5 Mold it into a round form or mound and cover it with a clean dish towel to let it rise.

6 After 30 minutes, knead it again.

7 Dust your work surface with more flour. Roll the dough out using a rolling pin to make a pizza round, or, if you like, an organic or square shape also works just fine.

8 Preheat the oven to 350 degrees F.

9 Transfer your crust to a pizza stone and brush the crust with olive oil. Prebake for 8 minutes.

10 Raise the heat to 475 degrees F. Add your toppings and bake for 8 to 10 minutes more.

CLASSIC LOW-GLUTEN PIZZA CRUST

MAKES TWO 8-INCH ROUNDS I use an OO organic flour in this recipe along with low-gluten oat flour. This dough works well for any pizza recipe in this section.

INGREDIENTI

1 cup 00 white organic flour, plus extra for dusting the work surface

1 cup oat flour

1 cup oat flour starter (page 86)

1 cup 00 white organic starter (page 86)

2 tablespoons olive oil, plus more for brushing

1 teaspoon Celtic sea salt

PREPARAZIONE

1 Add a handful of flour to a work surface or large cutting board.

2 Turn the white organic flour and the oat flour out on the surface and make a well in the center. Add both starters, the olive oil, and the salt.

3 Start to incorporate the dough using your hands and working from the outside in until a dough starts to form.

4 Knead the dough with the heels of your hands, turning it over until it becomes smooth to the touch.

5 Mold it into a round form or mound and cover it with a clean dish towel to let it rise.

6 After 30 minutes, knead it again.

7 Dust your work surface with more flour. Roll the dough out using a rolling pin to make a pizza round, or, if you like, an organic or square shape also works just fine. Who said pizza has to be round?

8 Preheat the oven to 350 degrees F.

9 Transfer your crust to a pizza stone and brush the crust with olive oil. Prebake the crust for 8 minutes.

10 Raise the heat to 475 degrees F. Add your toppings and bake for 8 to 10 minutes more.

HAILEY'S CAULIFLOWER PIZZA CRUST

MAKES ONE 13-INCH ROUND You may never taste a more delicious gluten-free crust. The texture is a little more like a pancake than a traditional crust, but this is a flavorful base for any combination of pizza toppings. You may have to eat your cauliflower-crust pizza with a fork, but you'll devour it all the same!

Hailey Louks is the creator of the food blog *Come Cook with Us*. Based in Malibu, she has been creating recipes for healthy eating with a focus on food freedom while loving your body, heart, and spirit.

INGREDIENTI

1 small cauliflower, chopped into small pieces

2 tablespoons coconut oil

1/2 cup light or full-fat coconut milk

5 tablespoons arrowroot

1 teaspoon Celtic sea salt

1/2 cup white rice flour

1   Preheat the oven to 350 degrees F.

2   Place the cauliflower pieces in the bowl of a food processor and pulse to make cauliflower "rice" (pulsing them in a blender works too). Set aside in a bowl.

3   Heat 1 tablespoon coconut oil in a large skillet over medium heat. Once the oil is hot, transfer the cauliflower rice to the pan and cook for 5 minutes, stirring occasionally. Return the cauliflower rice to a large bowl and set aside.

4   In a separate skillet, heat the remaining 1 tablespoon of coconut oil. Add the coconut milk and let cook for 2 minutes. Now add the arrowroot and mix to combine. The mixture will be chunky, but that is okay! Remove from the heat. Pour the mixture into the bowl of a food processor and blend until smooth. Then transfer the mixture back to the pan and continue to heat over medium heat for 5 minutes more, or until it thickens.

5   In the bowl with the cauliflower, put the thickened mixture, salt, and rice flour. Mix to combine. It should come together to form a thick dough. Use your hands to knead the dough well.

6   Transfer the dough to a greased pizza pan and smooth it out with a rolling pin to make one large pizza. You can also divide the dough to make smaller pizzas (there should be enough to make four small pizzas). Bake in the oven for about 30 minutes, or until golden brown.

7   Remove from the oven and add the desired toppings.

CLASSIC FAMILY-STYLE PIZZA

MAKES 1 PIZZA An all-time family favorite, this pizza is devoured every time we make it. Topping pizza with salad brings a fresh and crispy aliveness. And the warm cashew cheese sauce will never leave you missing that unsatisfying, store-bought shredded vegan or dairy cheese.

INGREDIENTI

1 cup Beet Tomato Sauce (page 42)

1 cup Classic Cashew Cheese Sauce (page 59)

"Italian-ish" Multi-green Caesar with Avocado Balsamic Dressing (minus the cheese) (page 262)

Classic Low-Gluten Pizza Crust (page 90)

IN ANTICIPO:
Prepare the Beet Tomato Sauce, Cashew Cheese Sauce, and "Italian-ish" Multi-green Caesar with Avocado Balsamic Dressing ahead of time, but do not dress the salad yet.

PREPARAZIONE

1   Preheat the oven to 475 degrees F.

2   Roll out the pizza dough and, using your hands, press it into a large round, oval, or square shape to fit your metal or clay baking stone.

3   Bake the pizza crust for 8 minutes. Lift out the pizza stone and crust from the oven using protective gloves (pizza stones are extremely hot!). Place it on a heatproof surface. Reduce the oven temperature to 400 degrees F.

4   Pour the tomato sauce into the center of the crust and, using a circular motion, spread it out so it is 1/2 inch from the outer edge of the crust. Spoon dollops of cashew sauce over the crust to cover well.

5   Bake the pizza for 8 minutes more, until it is piping hot.

6   Toss the salad with the dressing.

7   Remove the pizza from the oven using protective gloves. Using tongs, top the pizza with "Italian-ish" Multi-green Caesar salad. Devour!

PIZZA MARGHERITA

MAKES 1 PIZZA Beautifully simple, vibrant, and fresh. The cashew mozzarella rules!

INGREDIENTI

1 Spelt Pizza Dough (page 88)

2 tablespoons olive oil

1 cup Mathis's Simply Red Tomato Sauce (page 44)

1 Roma tomato, sliced

12 Mozzarella Balls in Brine (page 78)

Fresh basil leaves

1 tablespoon balsamic vinegar

Freshly cracked black pepper to taste

PREPARAZIONE

1   Preheat the oven to 475 degrees F.

2   Roll out the pizza dough. Drizzle with 1 tablespoon olive oil.

3   Pour the tomato sauce in the center of the crust and spread it out to the outer edges using a circular motion.

4   Arrange the tomato slices on the pizza.

5   Add the mozzarella balls on top—arranging them so that each pizza slice holds two balls of mozzarella.

6   Top with fresh basil leaves and drizzle with the vinegar and the remaining 1 tablespoon of olive oil.

7   Bake the pizza for 10 to 15 minutes on a pizza stone, until the crust is brown and the cheese is beginning to melt.

8   Garnish with freshly cracked pepper. Enjoy!

GORGONZOLA FIG ARUGULA PIZZA

MAKES ONE 13-INCH PIZZA An absolutely mouthwatering combination of deliciousness. For this pizza, you make a fig remoulade to slather on your pizza crust and then top it with arugula, more figs, onions, and garlic gorgonzola cheese. You can use any crust with this recipe, but I love it with Hailey's Cauliflower Pizza Crust. Bake the crust first, then cook the ingredients for the toppings and build the pizza. It's a beauty.

INGREDIENTI

10 large figs, halved

3 tablespoons olive oil

1 sweet onion, sliced

2 garlic cloves

2 cups wild arugula

1 teaspoon Celtic sea salt

1 baked Hailey's Cauliflower Pizza Crust (page 92)

1 cup Creamy Garlic Gorgonzola (page 56)

Freshly cracked black pepper to taste

PREPARAZIONE

1. Preheat the oven to 350 degrees F.

2. Place the figs on a rimmed baking sheet and roast for 5 to 8 minutes, until their juices release.

3. Heat 1 tablespoon of the olive oil in a cast-iron skillet over medium heat and add the onion slices. Sauté for about 5 minutes, until browned.

4. In the pitcher of a Vitamix or high-speed blender, place half of the browned onions, 1 or 2 of the roasted fig halves, the garlic, and 1 tablespoon olive oil. Process on low speed until well blended.

5. In a separate bowl, toss the arugula with the remaining 1 tablespoon of olive oil and the salt.

6. Spread the fig remoulade evenly on the prepared pizza crust. Then arrange the dressed arugula on top of the pizza in a ring and place the baked figs on top. Top with more browned onions and dollops of gorgonzola. Garnish with pepper.

BUFFALO CAULIFLOWER, PINEAPPLE, AND PORCINI BACON PIZZA

MAKES ONE 13-INCH PIZZA Even though it is not a typical Italian variation, I feel called to offer this twist on an American favorite pizza combo.

INGREDIENTI

1 head of cauliflower

Celtic sea salt and freshly cracked black pepper to taste

2 tablespoons barbecue sauce

1 pineapple

1 tablespoon olive oil

1 baked Spelt Pizza Dough (page 88)

1 cup Sun-Dried Tomato Sauce (page 43), plus more to taste

Cashew Almond Mozzarella (page 64)

Porcini Bacon (page 109)

PREPARAZIONE

1 Preheat the oven to broil.

2 Cut off the stem and leaves of the cauliflower and steam the florets for about 12 minutes, until tender but still firm. Drain in a colander and place in a medium bowl. Season with salt, pepper, and barbecue sauce. Toss to coat. Set aside.

3 Remove the rind from the pineapple and slice the pineapple into rings. Place the rings on a rimmed baking sheet and broil for 10 minutes or until slightly charred.

4 Using a small paring knife, cut out and discard the cores of the pineapple rings.

5 Reduce the oven temperature to 425 degrees F.

6 Drizzle the olive oil evenly over the baked crust. Pour the tomato sauce into the center of the crust and spread it to the outer edges using a circular motion.

7 Slice the block of mozzarella into 1/8-inch-thick slices. Arrange the slices of mozzarella so that each slice of pizza gets two pieces (I achieve this by making an outer ring of cheese over the whole pizza and then an inside ring).

8 Arrange the pineapple slices in a floral pattern. Add the cauliflower and arrange it to cover the pizza.

9 Top with pieces of porcini bacon.

10 Bake the pizza on a pizza stone for about 10 minutes, until it is heated through and the cheese melts.

PORCINI BACON

MAKES ABOUT 1 CUP Smoky and sweet notes are infused into mushrooms in this healthier and more compassionate way to satisfy your bacon craving.

INGREDIENTI

2 cups dried porcini mushrooms

1 tablespoon Bragg Liquid Aminos

1 teaspoon maple syrup

½ teaspoon smoked paprika (optional)

2 teaspoons liquid smoke

IN ANTICIPO: **Place the mushrooms in boiling hot water in a small bowl and soak for 1 hour.**

PREPARAZIONE

1 Drain the mushrooms (you can reserve the liquid for another recipe).

2 In a small bowl, place the mushrooms, aminos, maple syrup, paprika, if using, and the liquid smoke. Stir to coat.

3 Arrange in a single layer on a nonstick dehydrator sheet. Dehydrate at 100 degrees F for 4 hours.

4 Remove from the dehydrator. Store in an airtight container for up to 2 weeks.

BELOVED

To know yourself—and moreover to love yourself. When you experience the state where you know yourself as your own Beloved, the world will meet you there and your life will become a living prayer.

How many of us have a loving relationship with ourselves? If we really observe our inner chatter, likely we will find that we have been engaged in a dialogue with our bodies that includes repeated negative self-talk. We are constantly telling ourselves that we are not the version we really want. "If only you were thinner, taller, had different color hair or eyes, lighter or darker skin, or fewer wrinkles, then I would like you better. Then I could love you more." Sound familiar?

If you were talking to a friend or young child in this manner, what do you suppose the consequences of repeatedly saying "You are not really the one I wanted" might be? This practice is hugely destructive and unloving and adds to unresolved emotional trauma that is at the heart of many imbalances in the ways we all relate to food. Addictions to food are attempts to suppress our emotions so we don't have to feel the pain and so we can avoid any immediate suffering.

We must take responsibility for changing our relationship to ourselves and for clearing these unresolved emotional traumas if we are to experience our most authentic self and life.

The only way out is through.

Establishing a deep and loving relationship with our bodies is a powerful action that rebirths us into remembering the love that we actually are. What if you were the most precious being you know? What if you honored yourself with the highest kindness, respect, honor, and gratitude no matter what you look like in this present moment. How about cultivating deep gratitude for your body and for its miraculous life force, whose functions are beyond comprehension?

Our bodies are truly temples for our soul. Training our minds with positive thoughts is like taking responsibility for an unruly child. We can develop an understanding that we actually are not our minds, emotions, or thoughts. Our true, divine mind resides within our hearts. The heart is the supreme intelligence, and we can deeply feel its communication to us, if we only pay attention. Eating plant rich purifies the body so we can begin to feel and receive our true heart intelligence.

DAILY PRACTICE

Sit in front of a mirror and gaze into your eyes. Trace your face with your fingers, covering every line, contour, and area of your face. Keep looking at yourself, cultivating the same level of care, nurturing, and love that you would offer a precious child. Say, "Thank you, my precious divine body, for providing me the opportunity to live this human life. You are a miracle of life and I am so grateful for you. I love you, I honor you, and I will protect you and care for you always." Start to take long, deep inhales followed by long, deep exhales. Imagine you are breathing through your heart and feel in love with yourself.

Beets in Mint Pesto
page 136

ANTIPASTI AND CONTORNI

PORTABELLA PARMA N'HAM CON MELONE

ELEGANT MELON CARPACCIO

TOMATO-BASIL BRUSCHETTA

SPINACH AND GARLIC

CLASSIC FERMENTED GARLIC FENNEL KRAUT

BELUGA LENTIL CAVIAR WITH CASHEW SEA CHEESE

BRUSSELS SPROUTS WITH BALSAMIC GLAZE

ROASTED RED PEPPERS

ROASTED ROSEMARY POTATOES WITH BLACK TRUFFLE OIL

ROASTED TURNIPS AND SUNCHOKES

BEETS IN MINT PESTO

BLACKENED BALSAMIC CAULIFLOWER

TURNIP CAULIFLOWER ARTICHOKE MASH

ROASTED ARTICHOKES WITH CASHEW HERB CREAM

CASHEW HERB CREAM

PARMESAN EGGPLANT SQUASH POLENTA

RADICCHIO HERB SAUTÉ

TURNIP PESTO PANINI STACK

CANNELLINI BEANS WITH SWISS CHARD IN PISTACHIO OIL

PORTABELLA PARMA N'HAM CON MELONE

SERVES 4 When dehydrated, this woodland mushroom has a cool, thin, stretchy texture that is very close to the feel of the cured hams of Italy. The aminos add that unique salty flavor. You'll be shocked by how much this dish tastes like the traditional Italian appetizer, and you'll feel good knowing your food choices are doing good in the world.

INGREDIENTI

4 large portabella
mushrooms,
sliced 3/8 inch thick

4 tablespoons Bragg
Liquid Aminos

1 ripe Tuscan cantaloupe

1   Place the portabella mushroom slices in rows on a dehydrator tray.

2   Add the aminos, covering well to coat.

3   Place the dehydrator tray in the dehydrator and dehydrate at 100 degrees F for 4 hours, or until the mushrooms are stretchy and salty. If you over-dehydrate the portabellas or cut them too thin, they will be dry.

4   Slice the melon in half, remove the seeds and the rind, and place on a plate. Top with slices of the dehydrated portabellas. (Or remove the melon right from the rind using a spoon or small melon ball scooper and place the portabella slices on top of the melon balls.)

ELEGANT MELON CARPACCIO

SERVES 4 Elegance in simplicity. You can use a Tuscan cantaloupe in place of watermelon if you like. After you have shaved a few slices off your melon facade and it starts to contour in, use a sharp knife and cut off a section so that you have a clean, flat surface to continue shaving slices from.

INGREDIENTI

1 small ripe red or orange watermelon

1 teaspoon smoked salt
¼ cup fresh local sprouts

PREPARAZIONE

1 Cut the melon in half.

2 Using a sharp cheese slicer, shave off paper-thin ribbons of melon and arrange them on a pretty plate.

3 Garnish with the smoked salt and fresh sprouts.

TOMATO-BASIL BRUSCHETTA

SERVES 4 TO 6 One of the best ways to feature fresh ripe tomatoes is in this classic antipasti. I like to use heirloom tomatoes for their taste and color variety.

INGREDIENTI

1 red heirloom tomato, quartered and seeded

1 yellow heirloom tomato, quartered and seeded

20 fresh basil leaves

2 garlic cloves, peeled and coarsely chopped

¼ cup olive oil

2 teaspoons Celtic sea salt

1 teaspoon freshly cracked black pepper

Rustic bread, toasted, for serving

1   In the bowl of a food processor, place all of the ingredients except the bread.

2   Pulse eight times, or until the tomatoes are in about ¼-inch pieces. Do not overprocess the mixture or your bruschetta will become salsa.

3   Transfer the mixture to a glass container and store overnight if you can. I find bruschetta always tastes better the following day, when the flavors have had time to meld together. (Of course if you don't have time, you can eat it right away!)

4   Serve on top of toasted rustic bread.

SPINACH AND GARLIC

SERVES 4 TO 6 Sautéed spinach and garlic is a classic Italian, plant-powered veggie dish. With fresh produce and a large serving of love, it nourishes the soul. Serve this alongside Roasted Rosemary Potatoes with Black Truffle Oil (page 132).

INGREDIENTI

¼ cup sunflower seeds

2 tablespoons extra-virgin olive oil

8 cups fresh spinach

2 to 4 garlic cloves, chopped

1 teaspoon Celtic sea salt

PREPARAZIONE

1   Preheat the oven to 350 degrees F.

2   Arrange the sunflower seeds on a rimmed baking sheet and roast for 6 minutes, or until golden brown. Set aside.

3   In a medium saucepan or cast-iron skillet, heat the olive oil over medium heat. Add the spinach and garlic and sauté for 3 minutes, until the spinach is wilted.

4   Add salt to taste. Place the spinach mixture in a serving dish and sprinkle with the sunflower seeds.

CLASSIC FERMENTED GARLIC FENNEL KRAUT

MAKES ABOUT 2 CUPS Adding fermented kraut to your plate is an easy way to up the vibes in your gut. This version is popping with Italian flavors of garlic and fennel.

INGREDIENTI

1 medium head of green cabbage

1 large fennel bulb with stalks

1 medium bulb of fresh garlic

One 4-inch piece of fresh ginger

2 tablespoons fennel seeds

4 tablespoons Celtic sea salt

PREPARAZIONE

1   Slice the cabbage into very thin threads with a sharp knife. Discard the core and hard stems at the bottom of the outer leaves.

2   Slice the fennel finely, including the tops. Discard the bottom end piece.

3   Peel and finely chop or press the garlic.

4   Remove the skin from the ginger. Finely grate the peeled ginger.

5   In a 1-gallon glass container, layer the ingredients one a time, sprinkling generously with salt between the veggie varieties.

6   Fill a large mason jar with water and place the lid on tight. Weight the ingredients down by placing the mason jar on the top of the veggies inside the 1-gallon glass container.

7   Water should start to appear as the moisture releases from the veggies. Add more filtered water until it just covers the veggies.

8   Place a clean kitchen towel on top of the jar and secure it with a rubber band.

9   Place the glass container inside a dark cabinet for 2 to 3 weeks. Check on your kraut every few days, and skim off any black mold that appears on the top layer and discard. This happens when air contacts the veggies.

10   Transfer the fermented kraut to mason jars and store them in the fridge for up to 4 weeks. Leave about 1 cup behind in the jar and get started on your next batch.

BELUGA LENTIL CAVIAR WITH CASHEW SEA CHEESE

SERVES 4 Reminiscent of the delicacy caviar, this playful spin pairs lentils with Cashew Sea Cheese. I love to add a bit of chopped seaweed to give it that salty ocean taste.

INGREDIENTI

Beluga Lentil Caviar:

4 tablespoons apple cider vinegar

1 teaspoon Celtic sea salt

2 tablespoons olive oil

2 cups black beluga lentils

2 garlic cloves

1 bay leaf

2 tablespoons chopped dulse seaweed

4 radicchio leaves

Cashew Sea Cheese:

1 cup cashews

Juice of 1 small lemon

1 teaspoon tamari

Fresh chives, for garnish

IN ANTICIPO: Place the cashews in filtered water in a small bowl. Cover and refrigerate overnight.

PREPARAZIONE

1   In a medium bowl, combine the vinegar, salt, and olive oil. Add the radicchio leaves, turning them in the marinade. Let the radicchio marinate in the dressing for 15 minutes. Remove the radicchio leaves and set them aside, reserving the dressing for the lentils.

2   In a medium saucepan, bring 2 cups of water and the lentils to a boil over high heat. Add the garlic and bay leaf. Reduce the heat to medium and continue cooking until the lentils are tender and most of the water has been absorbed. Remove the saucepan from the heat and drain the lentil mixture. Discard the bay leaf.

3   Add the lentils and seaweed to the dressing mixture. Stir to combine well.

4   Drain the cashews. In the bowl of a food processor, place the drained cashews, lemon juice, and tamari. Process until smooth and creamy.

5   Arrange one radicchio leaf in the center of each of four serving plates. Spoon a large serving of lentils into the center of the radicchio. Using an ice-cream scoop, place a mound of Cashew Sea Cheese on top of the lentils. Place 5 long, thin chives in the center of the cheese.

BRUSSELS SPROUTS WITH BALSAMIC GLAZE

SERVES 6 This recipe is wonderfully rustic with its smoky flavors. The contrast of the salty taste of the tempeh bacon against the acid and sweetness of the balsamic vinegar gives the usually bland Brussels sprouts a delicious and lively taste. I find that halving the Brussels sprouts allows the flavors to penetrate more successfully.

INGREDIENTI

15 Brussels sprouts, halved
(unless they are very small)

¼ cup balsamic vinegar

2 teaspoons coconut oil

8 slices tempeh bacon

2 tablespoons olive oil

1 teaspoon Celtic sea salt

PREPARAZIONE

1 Heat a cast-iron skillet over high heat until hot. Add the Brussels sprouts to the pan (do not add oil).

2 Blacken the Brussels sprouts while stirring them occasionally. When they are slightly blackened and the green color has brightened, add ¼ cup of water and cover the pan with a tight-fitting lid. Cook for 4 to 6 minutes, until they are tender or until a fork inserted slides in easily.

3 In a small saucepan over low heat, add the vinegar and reduce, stirring constantly for 8 minutes, until it coats the back of a spoon.

4 Drain the Brussels sprouts and transfer them to a serving bowl.

5 Heat the cast-iron skillet over high heat and add the coconut oil.

6 Add the tempeh to the skillet and sauté until heated through. Remove the tempeh from the pan and slice it into small pieces.

7 Add the tempeh to the Brussels sprouts. Drizzle with the balsamic glaze, olive oil, and salt to taste. Toss to coat.

ROASTED RED PEPPERS

MAKES 2 CUPS This is a simple recipe for roasting your own red peppers. You'll need a gas burner or a grill. It takes only 15 minutes, and the jarred red peppers you can find at the market just don't compare. Using local organic peppers highlights the beauty of whole food as medicine. Red peppers are extremely high in vitamin C, making them healers in their own right.

INGREDIENTI

4 local red bell peppers, de-stemmed, seeded, and cut into quarters

2 tablespoons virgin olive oil

2 tablespoons balsamic vinegar

1 teaspoon Celtic sea salt

Freshly cracked black pepper to taste

PREPARAZIONE

1   Using tongs, place a section of the bell pepper skin-side down over an open flame. The bell pepper will be fine resting on a burner over an open flame or on the grill of a gas barbecue. Check the bell pepper frequently and roast it until the skin slightly blackens. This will take only 4 to 6 minutes. Remove the bell pepper from the flame and repeat with the other sections.

2   On a cutting board, slice the bell peppers in uniform sections lengthwise.

3   In a serving bowl, place the olive oil, vinegar, and salt and combine. Add the bell peppers to the marinade and stir to coat.

4   Transfer the bell peppers to a glass storage container, or use them in the Tree of Life Salad (page 248).

ROASTED ROSEMARY POTATOES WITH BLACK TRUFFLE OIL

SERVES 6 Nothing feels more nourishing in the belly than some hearty roasted potatoes. We like to roast them on a bit higher heat with generous amounts of coconut oil, sea salt, and pepper during the beginning stages of roasting. As they start to brown, we add slices of shallots and finely chopped rosemary for the final fifteen minutes of cook time. The truffle oil is an absolutely delicious contrast to the warm flavors of this dish.

INGREDIENTI

15 small golden potatoes, cut into 1/2-inch pieces

4 tablespoons refined or unscented coconut oil, melted

1 tablespoon Celtic sea salt

1 teaspoon freshly cracked black pepper

2 shallots, thinly sliced

2 tablespoons fresh rosemary, finely chopped

Black truffle oil, for drizzle

PREPARAZIONE

1   Preheat the oven to 425 degrees F.

2   Arrange the potatoes on a rimless baking sheet in one layer. Distribute the coconut oil evenly over the potatoes. Season with the salt and pepper and roast for 30 minutes.

3   As the potatoes start to brown, turn them over using a flat metal spatula. Lay the shallots and rosemary over the potatoes. Continue to bake for 10 to 15 minutes more.

4   Remove the potatoes from the oven and arrange them on a serving platter. Adjust the salt and pepper to taste. Drizzle with the truffle oil.

Note: If you want a healthier dish, reduce the coconut oil to 2 tablespoons and substitute truffle-infused salt for the truffle oil (omit the Celtic sea salt).

ROASTED TURNIPS AND SUNCHOKES

SERVES 4 TO 6 Roasting seasonal vegetables is a great way to honor whole food as designed by nature. I love the beauty in the simplicity of this dish, and I like to create it by using veggies that may be a little less familiar. Note: Sunchokes are sometimes referred to as "Jerusalem artichokes." Turnips are a wonderful vegetable that most people don't cook with, likely because they don't know how to prepare them. Of course, you can add any root vegetable to this mix, and you can use a variety of oils—olive, pistachio, or walnut oil. Serve this right out of the oven on a rustic cutting board and let everyone dig in!

INGREDIENTI

2 large turnips, well rinsed

4 sunchokes, well rinsed

2 teaspoons truffle salt

¼ cup hazelnut oil

PREPARAZIONE

1   Preheat the oven to 425 degrees F. On a wire rack, place the turnips and sunchokes with their skins on. Roast them for 40 to 60 minutes, until they are tender and soft to the touch.

2   Using oven mitts, remove the veggies from the oven and arrange them on a rustic cutting board. Slice them open and sprinkle them with the truffle salt. Drizzle the hazelnut oil over the top, seasoning with more salt to taste.

BEETS IN MINT PESTO

SERVES 4 TO 6 Food as art. This refreshing pesto is a nice change of taste in the warmer months of the year. Experiment using different varieties of oil such as avocado, pistachio, or almond oil. I like to reserve some whole oranges and fresh mint from the garden to create a beautiful presentation. Let the juice of the beets create an abstract effect on your plate.

INGREDIENTI

1½ cups almonds

1 cup fresh chocolate mint, plus more for garnish

Juice of 1 orange, plus fresh orange slices for garnish

3 tablespoons hazelnut oil

Pinch of Celtic sea salt

4 red beets, boiled and peeled

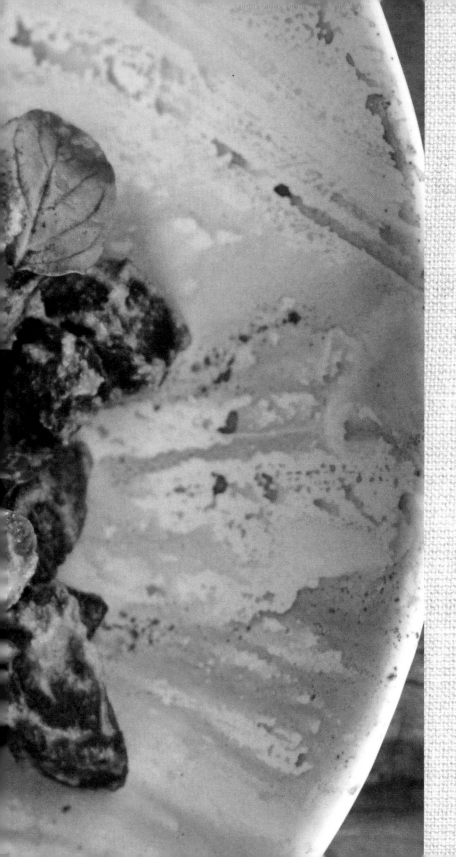

———
IN ANTICIPIO:
**Place the almonds in filtered water in a small bowl.
Cover and refrigerate overnight.**
———

PREPARAZIONE

1   Drain the almonds.

2   In the bowl of a Vitamix or high-speed blender, place the mint first, then the drained almonds, the orange juice, hazelnut oil, and salt. Blend on medium speed, using the plunger to distribute the mint. This will take a bit of patience. If the mixture is dry, you can add very small increments of filtered water (2 tablespoons at a time). Keep in mind that this is a pesto, so be careful not to make it too runny. Taste the pesto and adjust the salt. Transfer the mixture to a medium bowl.

3   Dice the beets into bite-size pieces. Toss them with the pesto.

4   Arrange fresh mint around the sides of a shallow bowl. Transfer the beets and pesto mixture to the center of the bowl and garnish with fresh orange slices.

BLACKENED BALSAMIC CAULIFLOWER

SERVES 4 TO 6 This is one of my favorite ways to serve cauliflower. It really comes alive with the contrast of the roasted fire and the sweet, acidic balsamic flavors. Garnished with your favorite Italian herbs, this is whole food at its very best. It is a great recipe to include as a side at dinner or a main at lunch. It also mixes beautifully into risotto and tastes delicious with roasted potatoes.

INGREDIENTI

2 heads of cauliflower

2 tablespoons olive oil

2 tablespoons Celtic sea salt

¼ cup balsamic vinegar

Freshly cracked black pepper to taste

Fresh oregano, rosemary, and thyme

PREPARAZIONE

1   Preheat the oven to broil.

2   On a baking sheet, place both heads of
    cauliflower stem-side down and brush them
    generously with olive oil. Sprinkle them with
    1 tablespoon of the salt.

3   Broil the heads of cauliflower until the tops
    become slightly blackened and the base of
    the cauliflower is a bit translucent and slightly
    tender. Remove the heads of cauliflower from
    the oven.

4   On a cutting board, cut off the heads and
    separate them into bite-size florets.

5   While they are steaming hot, arrange the florets
    on a serving plate and pour the vinegar over
    them. Sprinkle with the remaining salt and the
    pepper. Finish by sprinkling with fresh herbs.

TURNIP CAULIFLOWER ARTICHOKE MASH

SERVES 6 I adore this mash as a light, low-calorie substitute for potatoes. This trio seems to melt in your mouth. All of these veggies are high in vitamin C, which makes this a healthy choice as a side to your salad, pasta, or main.

INGREDIENTI

1 head of cauliflower

2 large turnips

1 teaspoon coconut oil

1 sweet onion, peeled and sliced thinly into rings

One 14.1-ounce can of artichoke hearts

1 tablespoon Celtic sea salt

1 teaspoon freshly cracked black pepper, plus more for garnish

1 Steam the entire head of cauliflower in a steamer for 25 minutes or until very soft. Remove the cauliflower and chop it into 2-inch pieces, discarding the stems and leaves.

2 Bring water to a boil in a small saucepan over high heat and boil the turnips for 30 minutes or until soft. Drain them in a colander. Leaving the skin on, chop the turnips into 2-inch pieces.

3 Heat the coconut oil in a cast-iron skillet over high heat. Add the onions and sauté them for 5 to 8 minutes or until browned. In the bowl of a food processor, place the cauliflower, turnips, half the onions, the artichoke hearts, salt, and pepper. Process until smooth.

4 Transfer the mash to a serving plate. Garnish with the remaining onions and pepper.

ROASTED ARTICHOKES WITH CASHEW HERB CREAM

SERVES 3 TO 6 This whole-food vegetable is best celebrated in its pure form. The herb cream is a welcome reprieve from the heat-producing garlic typical of dipping sauces. You will have to prepare it at least one day ahead.

INGREDIENTI

3 small artichokes   Cashew Herb Cream (page 144)

PREPARAZIONE

Boil the artichokes in a double boiler for about 40 minutes, until the leaves pull away easily. Serve with Cashew Herb Cream dipping sauce.

CASHEW HERB CREAM

MAKES ABOUT 2 CUPS A mild soft herbed cream that is a beautiful garnish to fresh whole veggies.

INGREDIENTI

2 cups cashews	1 tablespoon fresh oregano
3 tablespoons apple cider vinegar	1 tablespoon fresh thyme
1 teaspoon Celtic sea salt	1 teaspoon fresh lavender
¼ cup coconut milk	

IN ANTICIPO:

**Place the cashews in filtered water in a small bowl.
Cover and refrigerate overnight.**

PREPARAZIONE

1   Drain the cashews.

2   In the bowl of a Vitamix or high-speed blender, place the drained cashews, vinegar, salt, and coconut milk and blend on medium speed until smooth.

3   Transfer the mixture to the center of an 8-inch piece of fine cheesecloth. Gather the edges and tie them into a bundle with string.

4   Hang the bundle overnight or up to 48 hours. You can place a bowl underneath it to catch any moisture drips.

5   Transfer the mixture to a small bowl and fold in the oregano, thyme, and lavender.

PARMESAN EGGPLANT SQUASH POLENTA

SERVES 2 TO 4 Adding veggies to polenta makes for a hearty, savory side dish.

INGREDIENTI

1 cup polenta

1 small eggplant

1 butternut squash

1 cup Macadamia Parmesan (page 70)

Edible flowers, for garnish

PREPARAZIONE

1   Preheat the oven to 375 degrees F.

2   Prepare the polenta according to the package
    directions.

3   Bake the eggplant and squash whole on a wire
    rack in the oven for 40 minutes or until they are
    tender and soft to the touch.

4   Remove the eggplant and squash from the
    oven, slice them in half, and scoop out the
    insides. Discard the seeds and skins.

5   Add the eggplant, squash, and Macadamia
    Parmesan to the cooked polenta and stir to
    incorporate well.

6   Transfer the mixture to a serving bowl and
    garnish with edible flowers.

RADICCHIO HERB SAUTÉ

SERVES 4 TO 6 Radicchio is extremely bitter, so it's best sautéed over high heat in refined coconut oil, which helps break it down. Generous amounts of vinegar and Celtic sea salt are essential to cut the bitterness. If you like this extreme flavor contrast, you may start to crave this dish. Whole radicchio lettuce varieties provide a wonderful opportunity to showcase the whole food. This gorgeous lettuce proves the idea that nature does it best.

INGREDIENTI

1 teaspoon coconut oil

1 head radicchio

2 tablespoons olive oil

2 pints cherry tomatoes, stems removed

½ cup red wine

2 sprigs fresh rosemary

2 sprigs fresh oregano

2 sprigs fresh thyme

1 tablespoon balsamic vinegar

1 tablespoon apple cider vinegar

2 teaspoons large-grain Celtic sea salt

Freshly cracked black pepper to taste

PREPARAZIONE

1   In a large cast-iron skillet or wok, heat the coconut oil over high heat. Add the
     whole head of radicchio and sauté for about 3 minutes, turning, until slightly
     charred and wilted.

2   Transfer the radicchio to a serving platter. Using a small paring knife, cut out and
     chop the heart of the lettuce and the leaves into $\frac{1}{8}$-inch sections.

3   In a small saucepan over medium heat, place 1 tablespoon olive oil, the cherry
     tomatoes, and the chopped radicchio heart leaves and sauté for 1 minute.

4   Pour in the wine, cover with a tight-fitting lid, and simmer until the wine reduces
     down and the tomatoes soften.

5   Add the rosemary, oregano, and thyme and stir well.

6   Spoon the tomato mixture into the center of the head of radicchio and drizzle
     the leaves well with balsamic vinegar, apple cider vinegar, salt, and the remaining
     1 tablespoon of olive oil.

7   Adjust salt to taste and garnish with fresh ground pepper.

TURNIP PESTO PANINI STACK

SERVES 4 Using turnips as a foundational layer is a great gluten-free substitute for bread. Get creative and add any veggies or herbs that you fancy.

INGREDIENTI

2 turnips

2 teaspoons refined or unscented coconut oil

1 cup Almond Fennel Pesto (page 48)

Fresh basil leaves

Salt and freshly cracked black pepper

¼ cup Balsamic Glaze (page 126)

1   Rinse the turnips. Bring water to boil in a small saucepan over high heat and boil the turnips for 40 minutes or until tender.

2   Drain the turnips in a colander and rinse them in cold water. Remove the skins using your thumb to rub them off.

3   Slice the turnips into 1/8-inch-thick slices.

4   Heat the coconut oil in a cast-iron skillet over high heat. Add the turnips and brown on each side for about 5 minutes, until the markings of the turnip are visible.

5   Create a tower by using one turnip slice as a base, followed by 2 tablespoons of the pesto and a basil leaf. Finish with another turnip slice and repeat two more times.

6   Sprinkle the tower with salt and pepper.

7   Drizzle with the balsamic glaze.

CANNELLINI BEANS WITH SWISS CHARD IN PISTACHIO OIL

SERVES 6 This tasty version of the Italian bean takes just minutes to prepare. It's great for a lunch entrée or as a side to grilled veggies or pasta. Any local green works beautifully in this dish. Just use additional amounts of vinegar to offset any bitterness. If you can't find fermented garlic, you can use fresh garlic. The pistachio oil gives it a special nutty flavor, but, as in all Italian cooking, a great olive oil will also work just fine.

INGREDIENTI

1 tablespoon olive oil

2 bunches of fresh local Swiss chard, chopped

2 tablespoons apple cider vinegar

1 teaspoon large-grain Celtic sea salt

3 tablespoons pistachio oil

2 fresh garlic cloves, pressed, or 4 fermented black garlic cloves

Two 15-ounce cans of cannellini beans drained and rinsed

½ shallot, thinly sliced

Juice of ¼ lemon

PREPARAZIONE

1   In a cast-iron skillet or pan, heat the olive oil over medium-high heat. Add the chard and sauté. Cook the chard only until the leaves wilt a bit and the color brightens. Do not overcook. Remove the chard from the skillet and transfer it to a large serving platter. Add the vinegar and ½ teaspoon salt to the chard. Toss to coat and arrange the chard in a mound in the center of the platter.

2   In a clean cast-iron skillet, heat 1 tablespoon of the pistachio oil over medium heat. Add the fresh garlic and stir to coat for 1 minute.

(If you are using fermented garlic, do not heat it with the pistachio oil. Instead, carefully peel the fermented garlic and slice it thinly. Set aside. You will use the slices as a garnish.)

3   Add the cannellini beans. Heat through and remove from the heat.

4   Distribute the garlic-and-bean mixture around the outside of the chard mound to form a ring. Garnish with the fermented garlic slices, if using, and shallot slices.

5   Squeeze lemon juice over the entire dish and sprinkle with the remaining $1/2$ teaspoon of salt.

6   Drizzle the remaining 2 tablespoons of pistachio oil over the beans.

FOOD FREEDOM

Divine Love is like the Sun—it shines on every living thing in creation without discrimination. You are loved unconditionally and eternally by this light and celebrated for the fact that you exist in a body at all, before any titles gained or achievements earned.

Human love is more like a business arrangement. In relationships, we take vows that dictate a certain agreement of behavior. The love will be given if we follow the rules of the agreement, but if that contract is broken, the love is then taken away.

We can find ourselves in sticky territory when we apply this to food choices. Judgment is a form of violence, and if we bring it into our kitchens we have given ourselves over to an unnatural, unloving state. Food is nourishment for our body temples and it is the reason we gather together with our families. In the highest essence, family meals can be a form of ceremony, seeped in gratitude, connection, and reverence for our loved ones, communities, and greater life.

Experience the power of practicing unconditional love and acceptance for every person no matter where they are in their journey. This means no matter what they are eating.

When I was able to release Rich to his process, without judgment of his food choices, he was left to make his own decisions around food and life. This powerful Jedi move was the catalyst for great transformation in our relationship.

Love people where they are and keep living your truth. Be a shining example of living authentically, whatever that means to you. Be a lantern that doesn't discriminate. Give light freely to all.

Human beings are divine fractals of source. We cannot know or understand the reasons for people's choices from our ego's vantage point. We must realize that we are all on our own unique paths and Divine Mother or the greater force that is breathing us will take care of life. Your interference in another's path, life, or food choices is not required.

Be unconditional love.

DAILY PRACTICE

Sit outside or by a window with sunlight. Feel the sun's rays shining on you and your environment, nourishing you with energy. Feel the brilliant, constant, radiant frequency fill your entire experience. Let go of any need to interfere with its light. Notice that it is shining on all life-forms without discrimination. Feel its unconditionally loving celebration for all life no matter the version, race, creed, color, sex, age, or political party.

Inhale deeply and hold it for as long as you can. Now exhale.

Let Go & Let Goddess. She's got this.

Ravioli
page 194

5

PASTA AND PRIMO

FAMILY POTATO AND CARROT LASAGNA

KING OYSTER SCALLOPS WITH BUTTER AND SAGE

PASTA WITH PORCINI AND CARAMELIZED ONION SAUCE

GARLIC PUTTANESCA SAUCE OVER INK RICE PASTA

SPAGHETTI SQUASH AND ANCIENT GRAIN PASTA

SPAGHETTI AND WOOD EAR CLAMS

BLACK BEAN PASTA WITH TOMATO PESTO

SPAGHETTI ARRABIATA

TRUFFLE CASHEW FETTUCCINE ALFREDO

RAVIOLI

GLUTEN-FREE AND DAIRY-FREE GNOCCHI

WILDFLOWER RISOTTO

LOBSTER MUSHROOM RISOTTO

SMOKED CHANTERELLE RISOTTO

PICCATA TWO WAYS

POLENTA PANINI

WHOLE ROASTED EGGPLANT WITH PARMESAN

POTATO FENNEL TARTE AU GRATIN

POLPETTE NAPOLETANE

CLASSIC EGGPLANT PARMESAN

FAMILY POTATO AND CARROT LASAGNA

SERVES 8 Making lasagna is a family affair around our house. We were searching for a gluten-free version and we had limited success using packaged rice lasagna noodles because they kept breaking apart. This recipe uses thin slices of potato in place of the noodles, which works beautifully. This dish is made up of three unique recipes, so we split up in the kitchen to prepare each of the elements. Then we gather around the pan and build the lasagna together.

INGREDIENTI

2 cups Cashew Almond Ricotta (page 68)

8 large golden potatoes

4 carrots

2 shallots

1 tablespoon olive oil, for greasing the pan

Celtic sea salt to taste

Freshly ground black pepper to taste

Fresh oregano

2 cups Black Pesto (page 45)

2 cups Sun-Dried Tomato Sauce (page 43)

Fresh basil, for garnish

IN ANTICIPO:

The Cashew Almond Ricotta is best prepared the day before.

PREPARAZIONE

1   Preheat the oven to 350 degrees F.

2   Using a mandoline and wearing a protective glove (never skip the glove!), slice the potatoes very thinly. They should be thin enough that they are a bit transparent.

3   Thinly slice the carrots and shallots into rings or round pieces.

4   Lightly oil the bottom and sides of a rectangular lasagna dish or pan.

5   Lay the slices of the potato so that they overlap until the entire surface is covered. Salt and pepper them well—the potatoes need a fair amount of seasoning.

6   Add a sparse layer of carrots, shallots, and oregano.

7   Place a dollop of the Cashew Almond Ricotta and one dollop of pesto about 1½ inches apart, making sure that you are distributing the mixtures evenly. These sauces will melt and spread during baking.

8   Pour a quarter of the tomato sauce on top, using a rubber spatula to spread it evenly.

9   Repeat another three times or until you run out of the ricotta and pesto.

10   Pour the remaining tomato sauce over the top, cover with foil, and bake for 40 minutes. Remove the foil and continue baking for another 10 minutes. Garnish with fresh basil.

KING OYSTER SCALLOPS WITH BUTTER AND SAGE

SERVES 4 TO 6 King oyster mushrooms are the sea scallops of the woodlands. You can find them at your local farmer's market or order them online.

INGREDIENTI

One 10-ounce package of linguini pasta

2 teaspoons coconut oil

4 king oyster mushrooms, sliced into ³/8-inch-thick rounds

2 tablespoons vegan butter

13 fresh sage leaves

Macadamia Parmesan (page 70)

Salt and freshly cracked black pepper to taste

PREPARAZIONE

1 Prepare the pasta according to the package directions.

2 Heat the coconut oil in a cast-iron skillet over medium-high heat and add the mushrooms. Cook the mushrooms on one side until browned, then flip and brown them on the other side.

3 Add the vegan butter and sage and stir to coat. Remove the skillet from the heat.

4 Drain the pasta in a colander and arrange it on a serving platter. Top with the mushroom mixture and sage leaves.

5 Pour any remaining vegan butter from the skillet onto the pasta and sprinkle with Macadamia Parmesan. Season with salt and pepper.

—

THE MAGNIFICENT UNIVERSE OF MUSHROOMS!

Mother Nature gave us tastes of the sea mirrored in the woodlands. I discovered these culinary delights from a German chef turned mushroom supplier at my local farmer's market. Every week, Dirk from LA FungHi would give me a new variety of mushroom and teach me the various qualities and benefits of healing mushrooms. He blessed me with his expertise and generosity. I learned so much from him, and I am thrilled to share these recipes with you in this section so that you can use them seasonally in place of seafood and even chicken.

—

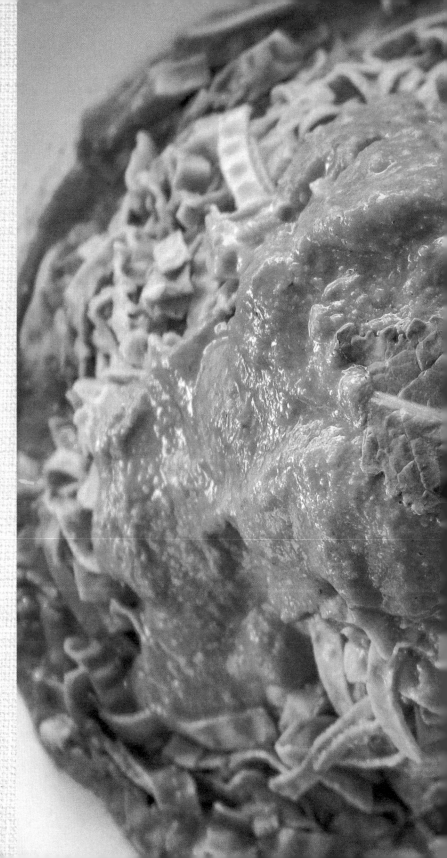

PASTA WITH PORCINI AND CARAMELIZED ONION SAUCE

SERVES 4 TO 6 Caramelized onions combined with woody notes of porcini make this sauce a fireside favorite.

INGREDIENTI

1 package pasta of choice

1 cup dried porcini

1 cup boiling water

2 tablespoons extra-virgin olive oil

1 small yellow onion, sliced

2 cloves fresh garlic, peeled and chopped

1 pint cherry tomatoes, halved, stems removed

1 cup red wine

5 sun-dried tomatoes in oil

2 tablespoons oregano

2 teaspoons salt

½ teaspoon black pepper

1 teaspoon maple syrup or agave

PREPARAZIONE

1   Bring a pot of water to boil on the stove and prepare the pasta according to package directions.

2   In a small bowl, steep the dried porcini mushrooms in the 1 cup boiling water for at least 20 minutes.

3   Heat the olive oil in a cast-iron skillet set over medium heat. Add the onions and sauté until golden, about 5 minutes. Add the garlic and sauté until the aroma of the garlic releases, about 2 minutes.

4   Add the cherry tomato halves and the wine, stirring to combine. Continue cooking until the wine reduces down.

5   In the pitcher of a Vitamix or high-powered blender, add the tomato mixture, sun-dried tomatoes, porcini mushrooms plus soaking liquid, oregano, salt, pepper, and maple syrup. Blend on high for 45 seconds.

6   Adjust the seasonings to taste. Pour over the prepared pasta and serve.

GARLIC PUTTANESCA SAUCE OVER INK RICE PASTA

SERVES 4 TO 6 Black rice pasta is the star of this twist on a classic favorite so we can leave our squid to do what they do best: frolic in the Mediterranean sea.

INGREDIENTI

¼ cup olive oil	½ cup olives
3 garlic cloves, peeled and chopped	½ cup caperberries
10 Roma tomatoes, seeded and quartered	1 to 3 teaspoons dried red pepper flakes
½ cup red wine	1 teaspoon Celtic sea salt
One 6-ounce can of tomato paste	Freshly cracked black pepper to taste
½ cup sun-dried tomatoes	One 12-ounce package black rice pasta

PREPARAZIONE

1. Heat the olive oil in a saucepan over medium heat and add the garlic. Sauté for 1 minute.

2. Add the tomatoes and stir to coat for 1 minute more.

3. Add the wine and simmer for 2 minutes.

4. In a small bowl, whisk the tomato paste with ½ cup of filtered water.

5. Add the tomato paste to the tomato mixture and continue to simmer for 8 minutes, or until the tomatoes soften but still keep their shape.

6. Add the sun-dried tomatoes, olives, caper berries, and red pepper flakes and stir well. Season with salt and black pepper.

7. Prepare the rice pasta according to the package directions. Do not overcook—keep it al dente!

8. Drain the pasta in a colander and transfer it to a serving dish. Pour the sauce over the pasta.

SPAGHETTI SQUASH AND ANCIENT GRAIN PASTA

SERVES 2 TO 4 I invented this dish as the perfect combination of healthy and hearty in a pasta dish—it's perfect when you want something a bit lighter but still satisfying.

Spaghetti squash is a natural whole-food pasta. It literally forms the noodles as you scoop it out of the gourd. Ancient grain pasta connects us to our ancestry. Together they make a great pair. The squash will be piping hot, so it's a perfect noodle for my raw tomato sauce.

INGREDIENTI

1 medium spaghetti squash

One 12-ounce package ancient grain pasta

1 cup pine nuts (pignoli)

2 tablespoons olive oil

2 teaspoons Celtic sea salt

Mathis's Simply Red Tomato Sauce (page 44)

Fresh basil to taste

Freshly cracked black pepper to taste

PREPARAZIONE

1   Preheat the oven to 350 degrees F.

2   Place the whole spaghetti squash on a wire rack
    in the oven and bake it for about 45 minutes, until
    soft to the touch.

3   When the squash is ready, bring a pot of water to a
    boil over high heat and prepare the ancient grain
    pasta according to the package directions.

4   Reduce the oven temperature to 325 degrees F.

5   On a rimmed baking sheet, lay out the pine nuts
    and bake for 8 minutes or until toasty brown.

6   Drain the ancient grain pasta and transfer it to a
    serving dish. Drizzle with the olive oil and sprinkle
    with ½ teaspoon salt.

7   When the spaghetti squash is soft to the touch, remove it from the oven and slice it in half.

8   Using a large spoon, run the spoon lengthwise down the cooked squash. The squash will come out in long spaghetti-like sections. Place the squash noodles over the ancient grain noodles.

9   Pour the tomato sauce over the noodles.

10   Garnish with the roasted pine nuts, basil, the remaining 1½ teaspoons of salt, and pepper.

SPAGHETTI AND WOOD EAR CLAMS

SERVES 4 Wood ear mushrooms are the clams of the forest. Paired with just the right amount of garlic, butter, and seasonings, you will find yourself satisfied with remembrances of the sea. Be careful when you sauté the mushrooms, as they will pop from the heat. Keep a safe distance and sauté only to heat through.

INGREDIENTI

One 16-ounce package organic gluten-free spaghetti

2 tablespoons olive oil

2 garlic cloves, sliced

2 cups fresh wood ear mushrooms

2 tablespoons vegan butter

1 teaspoon Celtic sea salt

2 tablespoons nutritional yeast

2 tablespoons tamari

1 bunch of flat-leaf parsley, coarsely chopped

PREPARAZIONE

1   Prepare the pasta according to package directions.

2   Heat the olive oil in a cast-iron skillet over medium heat and add the garlic. Sauté for 30 seconds.

3   Add the mushrooms and sauté for 1 minute more, being careful to stand back a bit, as the mushrooms can pop.

4   Add the vegan butter, salt, nutritional yeast, and tamari. Stir to coat and remove the skillet from the heat.

5   Drain the pasta in a colander and arrange in the center of a serving dish. Pour the mushroom mixture over the top.

6   Garnish with the parsley.

BLACK BEAN PASTA WITH TOMATO PESTO

SERVES 4 Black bean pasta is loaded with protein. When I eat a big bowl, I am always energized. Bean pasta really soaks up the salt content, so you have to add more seasonings than when you are cooking with regular pastas.

INGREDIENTI

3 heirloom tomatoes

One 6-ounce can of tomato paste

2 teaspoons fresh or dried oregano

1 teaspoon fresh or dried basil

3 sun-dried tomatoes, chopped

1 cup Almond Fennel Pesto (page 48)

One 12-ounce package black bean pasta

1 tablespoon olive oil

2 teaspoons Celtic sea salt

1/2 teaspoon fresh ground pepper

PREPARAZIONE

1. Bring 4 cups of water to a boil over high heat in a medium saucepan and add the heirloom tomatoes. Boil the tomatoes for 8 minutes or until their color brightens. Reduce the heat to low.

2. Remove ½ cup of the liquid from the pan and pour it into a small bowl. Add the tomato paste to the bowl and whisk until well incorporated.

3. Pour the tomato paste–water mixture back into the pan and stir well. Add the oregano and basil. Continue to cook for 5 minutes more.

4. Add the sun-dried tomatoes to the sauce and simmer for 5 minutes.

5. Stir in the pesto.

6. Prepare the pasta according to the package directions. Drain in a colander and rinse well. Transfer the pasta to a large serving bowl and add the olive oil. Toss to coat.

7. Pour the tomato sauce over the pasta and serve.

SPAGHETTI ARRABIATA

SERVES 4 The secrets to this delicious, full-bodied sauce are the red wine, heirloom tomatoes, and fresh red chili pepper. Adjust the kick to your liking. Finish with balsamic vinegar to get the full effect.

INGREDIENTI

One 8-ounce package organic ancient grain spaghetti

1 tablespoon olive oil, plus more to drizzle on the spaghetti

1 small shallot, finely sliced

1 to 2 teaspoons red chili pepper (depending on desired heat), finely chopped

2 red heirloom tomatoes, cut into wedges

1/2 cup red wine

One 6-ounce can of tomato paste

1 teaspoon dried red pepper flakes, plus more for garnish

1 1/2 teaspoons Celtic sea salt

2 tablespoons balsamic vinegar

1/2 teaspoon freshly cracked black pepper

PREPARAZIONE

1   Prepare the spaghetti according to the package directions.

2   Heat the olive oil in a saucepan over medium heat and add the shallot. Sauté until the shallot is soft and lightly brown.

3   Add the red chili pepper to the shallot and sauté for 30 seconds.

4   Add the tomatoes and sauté the mixture for about 1 minute, until the tomatoes start to soften.

5   Add the wine and let simmer for 3 minutes.

6   Add the tomato paste, red pepper flakes, salt, and ¼ cup water (or more for the desired consistency).

7   Drain the spaghetti in a colander and arrange it in a mound in the center of a serving plate. Drizzle the spaghetti with olive oil and, using tongs, incorporate the oil into the pasta, stirring in a circular motion.

8   Pour the tomato sauce over the top of the spaghetti.

9   Finish by drizzling with the balsamic vinegar and garnish with red pepper flakes and black pepper.

TRUFFLE CASHEW FETTUCCINE ALFREDO

SERVES 4 This is my third Alfredo sauce since I started creating plant-based recipes. It's difficult to say which one I like the best. They are all uniquely delicious. The genius of this version is in its simplicity. It also has a distinctive flavor that comes from the truffle salt. This is a great dish to make after a long day at the office or for a late-night plate after a night on the town. It takes only ten minutes.

INGREDIENTI

2 cups cashews

¼ cup nutritional yeast

1 teaspoon garlic powder

½ teaspoon white pepper

2 teaspoons truffle salt

One 8-ounce package of fettuccine noodles

Freshly cracked black pepper to taste

IN ANTICIPO:

**Place the cashews in filtered water in a small bowl.
Cover and refrigerate overnight.**

PREPARAZIONE

1   Drain the cashews.

2   Heat a large pot of water to a boil over high
    heat for the pasta.

3   In the bowl of a Vitamix or high-speed blender,
    add the drained cashews, nutritional yeast,
    garlic powder, white pepper, and truffle salt.
    Add 1 cup of hot water and blend on high
    speed for 1 minute or until smooth. Adjust the
    salt to taste and add more water, 2 tablespoons
    at a time, until the desired consistency is
    reached.

4   Prepare the pasta according to the package
    directions in the pot of boiling water. Drain the
    pasta in a colander.

5   Transfer the pasta to a serving platter and add
    the Alfredo sauce. Garnish with black pepper.

RAVIOLI

SERVES 4 These pillows of pasta are wonderful stuffed with fresh pesto. My daughter Mathis and I love to make this dish together. We use a basic hand-crank pasta machine she purchased for a school project. It works great, and the dough is "double O" perfect. This ravioli is not gluten-free, but it is organic. I like to use this specialty flour from Country Mills, an organic online source. Be careful that the water is not boiling too hard when you cook the ravioli, to prevent the ravioli from breaking.

INGREDIENTI

1½ cups 00 organic flour, plus extra for kneading and for dusting the work surface

¼ cup aquafaba (liquid from canned garbanzo beans)

¼ cup salted water

1 tablespoon olive oil

1 teaspoon Celtic sea salt

Cheesy Pesto (page 46)

Tomato sauce of your choosing

IN ANTICIPO:

Chill the aquafaba for 30 minutes.

PREPARAZIONE

1   Place the flour in a mound in the center of a large cutting board or work surface.

2   Create a large well in the center of the flour.

3   Pour a small amount of aquafaba and a small amount of salted water into the well. Add the olive oil and salt. Start working the flour with your hands, bringing it in from the outer edges. Keep incorporating the flour into the wet mixture, adding more aquafaba and salted water as you go.

4   If the dough is sticky, add a bit more flour and knead the dough while flipping and turning it.

5   Using the heel of your hand, keep working the dough for a good 15 minutes. You want the dough to become smooth.

6   Set the dough aside and cover it with a kitchen towel for 1 hour or more.

7   Cut the dough into four sections. Flour a pasta crank well. Flatten one section of the dough and feed it into the pasta machine, cranking it

and lifting the pasta through. Repeat twice on three settings of decreasing thickness (02, 03, and 04) until the dough is transparent. Repeat with the remaining three sections. Set the dough aside (keep covered it until ready to use).

8   Lay flat one of the large sheets of dough and place dollops of the pesto filling about 2 inches apart.

9   Brush the edges of the dough and in between each filling with aquafaba. Add a top sheet of dough, pressing the edges together and pressing in between each filling.

10   Repeat with the other two sheets of dough.

11   Using a pasta knife, cut between the fillings to cut out your ravioli. Sprinkle them lightly with flour so they do not stick together when they cook.

12   Bring a large pot of water to a boil over high heat and add the ravioli one at a time. Boil them over low heat for 3 to 5 minutes, until done.

13   Smother the ravioli with your favorite sauce.

GLUTEN-FREE AND DAIRY-FREE GNOCCHI

SERVES 4 Making gnocchi is so easy and fun that it's a great place to start when you are learning how to make pasta. The potato-and-flour mixture already holds together nicely from the natural starch in the potatoes, so any gluten-free flour you like will work well in this recipe. Keep kneading the dough for at least 15 minutes to get rid of the lumps. You can use a grooved wooden pasta board to create your gnocchi shape, or using a fork will work too.

INGREDIENTI

2 medium yellow potatoes (about 2 cups)

¼ cup organic fine corn flour, rice flour, or other gluten-free flour, plus extra for kneading and rolling

1 tablespoon nutritional yeast

1 tablespoon olive oil, plus more for drizzling

1 teaspoon Celtic sea salt

1½ cups Mathis's Simply Red Tomato Sauce (page 44)

½ cup Macadamia Parmesan (page 70)

1 bunch of fresh basil, thinly sliced

Freshly cracked black pepper to taste

PREPARAZIONE

1 Peel the potatoes. Bring water to a boil over high heat in a medium saucepan and add the potatoes. Boil them for about 30 minutes, until they are tender when a fork is inserted. Drain the potatoes and let them cool.

2 On a large cutting board or work surface, dice the cooked potatoes until the pieces are very small.

3 Add the flour, nutritional yeast, olive oil, and salt to the potatoes.

4 Combine the mixture with your hands and knead until the mixture forms a dough. Keep kneading the dough, flipping it over and turning it for about 15 minutes, until all the lumps are removed.

5 Add a handful of flour to the work surface. Divide the dough into four sections.

6 Using both hands, roll each section into a long, cord-size piece about 16 inches long. Cut the cords into ½-inch pieces.

7 Roll the ½-inch pieces between your hands and gently place them on the wood pasta board. Make a slight indentation with your thumb and roll them gently into a gnocchi shape using the grooved wooden pasta board or the tines of a fork. Repeat with the other sections of dough.

8 Bring a large pot of water to a boil over high heat. Carefully add the gnocchi and boil for just a few minutes, until they float to the top of the water.

9 Drain the gnocchi in a colander. Transfer them to a serving plate and drizzle them with olive oil.

10 Pour the tomato sauce over the gnocchi and sprinkle with Macadamia Parmesan.

11 Garnish with basil and pepper.

WILDFLOWER RISOTTO

SERVES 8 This risotto is a sweet return to the days of flower power. Garnished with edible flowers and sweet honey, it's a great addition to any brunch. I use traditional Arborio rice to get an extra-creamy texture. The cheesy flavor comes easily with a generous amount of nutritional yeast. Extra benefit: it's packed with B vitamins.

INGREDIENTI

1 medium butternut squash

½ cup nutritional yeast, plus more as needed

2 large garlic cloves

¼ cup plus 2 teaspoons olive oil

2 teaspoons large-grain Celtic sea salt, plus more as needed

3 cups Arborio rice

5 sprigs of fresh thyme

Freshly ground black pepper to taste

1 cup edible flowers, for garnish

2 tablespoons honey or maple syrup

PREPARAZIONE

1   Preheat the oven to 350 degrees F.

2   Bake the whole butternut squash on a wire
    rack in the oven for 45 minutes or until soft
    and brown.

3   After the squash cools enough to be handled,
    remove the skin and the seeds and place
    4 cups of the flesh in the bowl of a Vitamix or
    high-speed blender (save the rest for a soup).
    Add the nutritional yeast, garlic, ¼ cup of the
    olive oil, 1 cup of filtered water, and the salt
    and blend on high speed for at least 1 minute.
    Set aside.

4   Heat the remaining 2 teaspoons of olive oil over
    medium-high heat in a large, flat Le Creuset
    or other enameled pan that is at least 2 inches
    deep. Add the rice and sauté until all the
    kernels are coated with oil. Add filtered water
    to cover the rice by 1½ inches.

5 Stir the rice constantly until the water is absorbed into the rice. Then add more water in 1-cup increments and keep stirring until the water is absorbed. Reduce the heat to medium-low. Keep stirring and adding more water in 1-cup increments for about 40 minutes, until the rice is creamy, thick, soft, and moist.

6 Remove the rice from the heat. Fold the squash mixture into the rice, stirring it until the risotto is completely yellow in color.

7 Taste the risotto and adjust the salt and nutritional yeast. Be generous here because the rice soaks up the flavorings.

8 Strip 2 sprigs of thyme and sprinkle the leaves over the risotto. Add the pepper.

9 Garnish the risotto with the edible flowers. Place the 3 remaining sprigs of thyme in the center of the risotto. Serve the risotto in the pan. Drizzle with honey to finish. Or, if you want a vegan option, try maple syrup.

LOBSTER MUSHROOM RISOTTO

SERVES 8 I've caused outrage when I've posted photos of this dish because people thought I was using actual lobster. But the "lobster" in this recipe actually refers to a woodland variety, not the ancient creature that scours the seafloor. I get it. It is mind-blowing. Lobster mushrooms are available fresh only during the fall season, but you can also find them dried online. Not only is this iron-rich mushroom lobster orange, but it also smells of the sea! Mother Nature never ceases to delight me.

INGREDIENTI

2 tablespoons olive oil

16 ounces Arborio rice

1 cup kombucha or beer

¾ cup nutritional yeast,
plus more to taste

5 garlic cloves, finely chopped

2 cups lobster mushrooms, diced

2 teaspoons Celtic sea salt,
plus more to taste

1 teaspoon freshly cracked black pepper,
plus more to taste

1 Heat 1 tablespoon of the olive oil over medium-high heat in a large, flat Le Creuset or other enameled pan that is at least 2 inches deep. Add the rice and sauté until all the kernels are coated with oil. Add filtered water to cover the rice by $1\frac{1}{2}$ inches.

2 Stir the rice constantly until the water is absorbed into the rice. Then add more water in 1-cup increments and keep stirring until the water is absorbed. Reduce the heat to medium-low. Keep stirring and adding more water in 1-cup increments for about 40 minutes, until the rice becomes creamy, thick, and soft.

3 Pour in the kombucha and stir the rice until the kombucha is completely absorbed and the rice is very moist.

4 Add the nutritional yeast and stir to incorporate well. Remove the rice from the heat.

5 In a cast-iron skillet, heat the remaining tablespoon of olive oil over medium heat and add the garlic. Sauté until the garlic aroma releases. Now add the lobster mushrooms and sauté to coat.

6 Fold the mushrooms and garlic mixture into the rice. Sprinkle with the salt and pepper.

7 Adjust the seasonings to taste, adding more nutritional yeast in 1-tablespoon increments.

SMOKED CHANTERELLE RISOTTO

SERVES 8 A warm, savory, nourishing, and nurturing bowl of steaming risotto for the colder months. Chanterelles are healers packed with vitamin D and are great stand-ins for the sun on chilly and cloudy days. The smoky flavor of this risotto brings out the flavors and aromas best experienced in front of an inviting winter fire.

INGREDIENTI

2 tablespoons vegan butter

16 ounces Arborio rice

2 cups Smoked Walnut Parmesan (page 74)

2 garlic cloves, chopped

4 cups chanterelle mushrooms

2 tablespoons fresh oregano leaves

2 teaspoons garlic powder

2 teaspoons smoked salt, or
2 teaspoons liquid smoke
plus 2 teaspoons Celtic sea salt

Freshly cracked black pepper to taste

PREPARAZIONE

1 Heat 1 tablespoon of the vegan butter over medium-high heat in a large, flat Le Creuset or other enameled pan that is at least 2 inches deep. Add the rice and sauté until all the kernels are coated with vegan butter. Add filtered water to cover the rice by 1½ inches.

2 Stir the rice constantly until the water is absorbed into the rice. Then add more water in 1-cup increments and keep stirring until the water is absorbed into the rice. Reduce the heat to medium-low. Keep stirring and adding more water in 1-cup increments for about 40 minutes, until the rice becomes creamy, thick, and soft. Add in the Smoked Walnut Parmesan and stir to incorporate well.

3 In a cast-iron skillet over medium heat, heat the remaining 1 tablespoon of vegan butter and add the garlic. Sauté until the garlic aroma releases. Add the mushrooms and sauté to coat.

4 Fold the mushroom mixture into the rice. Sprinkle with the oregano, garlic powder, salt, and pepper.

5 Adjust the seasonings to taste.

PICCATA
TWO WAYS

SERVES 2 TO 4 When I think of Italian food, I often crave the distinct lemon flavor of piccata sauce in this hearty dish. I adore this sauce over chicken of the woods, or "chicken" mushrooms, which resemble white chicken breasts but hail from the woodlands. Isn't Mother Nature clever? These exotic mushrooms are a delicacy, and they are incredible to experience, but they may take some effort to find, as they are in season only in the fall months. For this recipe I offer tempeh as a delicious substitute.

INGREDIENTI

4 cups chicken of the woods mushrooms or 4 cups tempeh

4 tablespoons olive oil

8 garlic cloves, peeled and chopped

1 cup white wine

½ cup vegan butter

Juice of 1 large lemon

2 teaspoons Celtic sea salt

¼ cup capers

1 tablespoon arrowroot

¼ cup chopped fresh Italian parsley, plus more for garnish

8 cups fresh spinach

Picatta prepared with
chicken mushrooms

PREPARAZIONE

For Chicken Mushrooms:

Tear the chicken mushrooms into large strips. Heat a cast-iron skillet over medium-high heat. Add the chicken mushrooms and cook until blackened (do not use oil or liquid). Remove the mushrooms from the pan and arrange on a serving plate.

Proceed to step 3.

To maintain the similar texture of white chicken in this woodland mushroom, do not get it moist with oil or water.

For Tempeh:

———

IN ANTICIPO:

Place the tempeh in filtered water in a small bowl and soak for at least 1 hour.

———

1   Drain the tempeh, then cut it crosswise into 3-inch rectangles.

2   Heat a cast-iron skillet over medium-high heat. Add 1 tablespoon of olive oil and the garlic to the skillet and sauté the garlic until the aroma releases. Add the tempeh strips and cook, while turning, until browned. Transfer to a serving platter.

Picatta prepared with tempeh

3 Add 1 tablespoon olive oil and the remaining 4 garlic cloves, into a medium saucepan and sauté for 5 minutes over medium heat. Add the white wine, reduce the heat to low, and simmer for about 5 minutes, until the alcohol burns off. Add the vegan butter and stir until it melts into the wine mixture. Add the lemon juice, salt, and capers.

4 Spoon ¼ cup of the wine mixture into a small bowl and add the arrowroot. Whisk until well combined and free of lumps. Add this mixture back into the pan and whisk until it thickens.

5 Remove the pan from the heat and add in 2 tablespoons of the parsley.

6 In a large wok or cast-iron skillet, sauté the spinach in the remaining 1 tablespoon of olive oil for 3 minutes or until wilted. Using tongs, transfer the spinach to a large serving dish and make a bed of greens for the tempeh or mushrooms.

7 Arrange the tempeh or mushrooms over the spinach and pour the warm sauce over the dish just before serving. Garnish with the remaining parsley.

POLENTA PANINI

SERVES 4 Not your ordinary panini! These sandwiches make a delicious meal at lunchtime or late at night. A panini grill works great for this recipe, but if you don't have one, you can use a cast-iron skillet.

INGREDIENTI

4 cups polenta

2 to 4 tablespoons refined or unscented coconut oil, for grilling

4 tablespoons Olive and Sun-Dried Tomato Tapenade (page 50) (can be made up to 3 days ahead of time and stored in the refrigerator)

4 tablespoons Roasted Pine Nut (Pignoli) Spread (page 51) (can be made up to 3 days ahead of time and stored in the refrigerator)

4 fresh basil leaves

PREPARAZIONE

1 Prepare the polenta according to the package directions. Pour the polenta into a 9 x 9-inch pan and let it cool until it sets up and is firm. You may want to refrigerate the polenta to expedite the cooling process. Or prepare it a day ahead and store in the refrigerator.

2 Cut the polenta into 2 x 1½-inch rectangles or the size of small pieces of bread. If your polenta is very thick, you can cut it into cross-sectional slices so that you get thinner pieces. This size pan will yield about 8 pieces.

3 Heat the refined coconut oil on a panini grill or in a cast-iron skillet over high heat. Add the polenta and grill it on both sides. When it's done, the polenta will look glassy and appear to be moist and brighter yellow in color.

4   Place 1 polenta slice in the middle of a serving plate. Spread some tapenade on it. Top with another slice of polenta. Place about 1 tablespoon of the pine nut spread on the top and garnish with a single basil leaf. Repeat the process three more times.

5   Eat your panini with a fork and knife. And enjoy the health benefits of this gluten-free Italian sandwich.

WHOLE ROASTED EGGPLANT WITH PARMESAN

SERVES 4 Simply decadent. Whole, baked eggplants paired with Macadamia Parmesan is a heavenly match.

INGREDIENTI

4 whole baby eggplants

4 teaspoons olive oil

½ cup Macadamia Parmesan (page 70)

Freshly cracked black pepper to taste

1 Preheat the oven to 325 degrees F.

2 Pierce the eggplants with a fork and place them on a wire rack inside the oven. Bake for 40 minutes or until soft to the touch.

3 Using tongs, remove the eggplants from the oven and place them on a serving dish.

4 Slice each eggplant down the center to open it (like a baked potato) and drizzle each eggplant half with 1 teaspoon of olive oil.

5 Add 2 tablespoons of the Parmesan inside the eggplant and mix with a spoon to incorporate well.

6 Top with pepper and enjoy!

POTATO FENNEL TARTE AU GRATIN

SERVES 6 I was longing for a great gluten-free and vegan gratin recipe that I could serve for lunch during a band photo shoot at our house. It was a rainy day, but the creativity was flowing. My friends Jan and Lucy were taking pictures of my boys' band while I was simultaneously churning out new creations from the kitchen to be photographed by Leia. It was a delicious afternoon, a perfect combination of family, friends, and creativity. With its pretty scalloped pattern, this dish reminds me of a community of artists collaborating and creating together around food. A beautiful day.

INGREDIENTI

1 small fennel bulb, thinly sliced

1 small shallot, sliced

¼ cup olive oil, plus more
for greasing the pie pan

8 large golden potatoes

Celtic sea salt to taste

Freshly cracked black pepper to taste

2 cups Cashew Almond Ricotta
(page 68)

Fresh thyme to taste

Fresh oregano to taste

IN ANTICIPO:
Prepare the Cashew Almond Ricotta 1 day ahead.

PREPARAZIONE

1   Heat a cast-iron skillet over medium-high heat and add the fennel slices. Cook with no oil for about 8 minutes, until the fennel is slightly blackened. Set aside.

2   Using a protective glove, slice the potatoes on a mandoline in very thin slices so that when you hold them up, they are slightly transparent.

3   Preheat the oven to 350 degrees F.

4   Lightly oil a 10-inch ceramic pie pan with olive oil. Arrange the potato slices in a circular pattern, overlapping the slices to create a continuous layer across the bottom of the pan. Salt and pepper them well, adding shallot slices plus teaspoon-size dollops of the ricotta about 2 inches apart. Sprinkle with the thyme and oregano.

5   Continue in the same manner with another layer. Repeat two more times and finish with a potato-pattern top layer.

6   Brush the top with the ¼ cup of olive oil, making sure to cover the entire surface. Salt and pepper well. Cover with aluminum foil and bake for 45 minutes or until the potatoes are tender.

7   Remove the foil and bake for 8 minutes more or until the top is browned.

POLPETTE NAPOLETANE

SERVES 4 We enjoyed these patties smothered in fresh tomato sauce at a long table set in the fields of Tuscany. They are absolutely delicious.

INGREDIENTI

4 cups fresh spinach

2 cups boiled potatoes, peeled

1 cup almond flour

2 tablespoons arrowroot

2 teaspoons fresh grated ginger

1 teaspoon baking powder

2 teaspoons Celtic sea salt

Freshly cracked black pepper to taste

Extra-virgin olive oil

1 batch Mathis's Simply Red Tomato Sauce (page 44)

1 batch Smoked Walnut Parmesan (page 74)

IN ANTICIPO:

Prepare Mathis's Simply Red Tomato Sauce and the Smoked Walnut Parmesan ahead of time.

PREPARAZIONE

1. Bring water to a boil in a medium saucepan over high heat. Add the spinach and boil for about 1 minute, until wilted. Drain the spinach in a colander and set aside.

2. In a medium bowl, mash the potatoes with the cooked spinach, almond flour, arrowroot, ginger, baking powder, salt, and pepper until well incorporated.

3. Using your hands, form 2½-inch-round patties and set them on a plate next to the stove. You can prepare these ahead of time and refrigerate them until you are ready to sauté them.

4. Heat olive oil to coat the bottom of a large skillet over medium heat.

5. Add the patties and sauté on one side for 3 to 5 minutes, until they are golden brown, then turn and brown the other side.

6. Transfer the patties to a serving plate and smother them with the tomato sauce.

7. Drizzle with olive oil and garnish with the Parmesan and pepper.

CLASSIC EGGPLANT PARMESAN

SERVES 8 The four mouthwatering components of this recipe create a symphony of deliciousness. Say good-bye to your table manners when you enjoy this crowd-pleasing twist on an Italian classic—finger licking is unavoidable.

INGREDIENTI

1 batch Cashew Almond Ricotta (page 68)

3 large eggplants

2 teaspoons Celtic sea salt

1/4 cup olive oil

1 batch Almond Fennel Pesto (page 48)

1 batch Classic Cashew Cheese Sauce (page 59)

Fresh basil leaves

1 batch Beet Tomato Sauce (page 94)

IN ANTICIPO:

Make the Cashew Almond Ricotta 1 to 3 days in advance.

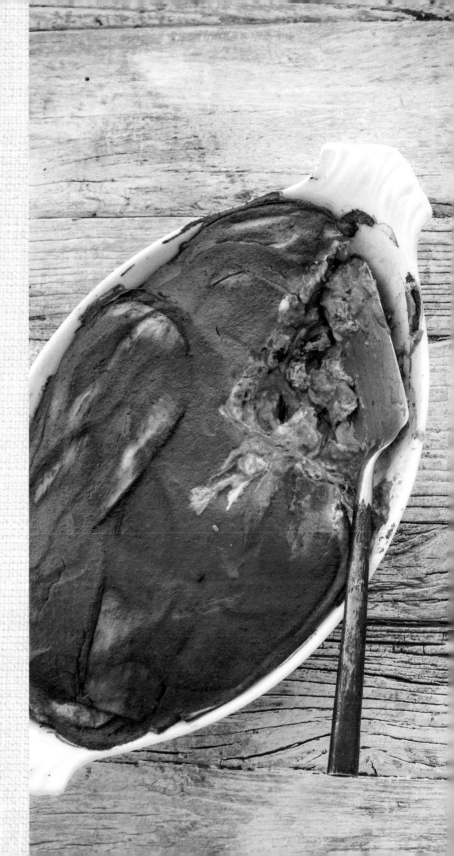

PREPARAZIONE

1. Cut off the stems of the eggplants and slice them crosswise to make large, flat slices, about ⅛ inch thick. You will need to discard (or compost) some smaller end and side pieces since you want larger slices with more surface area that will provide a good foundation for your layers.

2. Arrange the eggplant slices flat on unrimmed baking sheets and sprinkle with 1 teaspoon of salt. Let them stand for about 30 minutes. Then turn them and salt the other side with the remaining 1 teaspoon of salt and let them stand for 30 minutes more.

3. After the eggplant slices have been salted, they will release moisture. Blot each side well using a paper towel.

4. Preheat the oven to broil.

5. Drizzle the eggplant slices with 2 tablespoons of olive oil and broil for 4 to 6 minutes or until they are slightly charred. Do not overbroil or the eggplant slices will disintegrate and become too thin to use (start with 4 minutes on high and then watch them carefully). Remove the slices using a spatula, being careful not to tear them.

6   Reduce the oven heat to 375 degrees F.

7   Lightly oil a large shallow baking dish with 1 tablespoon olive oil and arrange the slices lengthwise, overlapping them slightly. Continue, covering the entire surface. Spoon 1 tablespoon of the pesto on top of the eggplant every 2 to 3 inches. Pour 1 tablespoon of the cashew sauce in between the pesto dollops, and place 1 tablespoon of the ricotta in the remaining open space.

8   Add a fresh basil leaf on top of each addition of the cashew sauce. Spread a quarter of the tomato sauce evenly over this first layer.

9   Add another layer of eggplant and repeat the steps above three or four more times, until you run out of eggplant or reach the top of the dish. Finish with an eggplant layer.

10   Pour the remaining tomato sauce over the entire surface, cover the dish with aluminum foil, and bake for 45 minutes. Remove the foil and bake for 8 minutes more or until the top is browned.

MUSIC AS A PRAYER

Music is a powerful healing force. Singing and sharing music is an important element of our retreat experience. I wrote "In the Sun" for Rich at a time when nothing seemed to be working in his life. He was beaten down and tired from struggling to survive in a career that was killing him emotionally, physically, and spiritually. He was raw, unsure, and vulnerable to life. As he struggled to find a way to move into serving his heart, and also provide for his family, it seemed that nothing was working. I witnessed his painful struggle and wrote this love song for him as a message of faith to keep on pursuing his dreams.

I feel that "In the Sun" is a love letter to us all to keep going, to have faith, and to believe that we are so much more than we know. Above all, serving our hearts' deepest desires is the only true mission of our soul. And if we stay the course, we will realize our true purpose.

It's been a long hard road
down the line
I've lost the truest part
of who I am

How much can one man take
nothing seems to stick
I've got to find my way
to be the one for you

You in the sun
In the morning
you are more than you know

Sometimes you gotta
lay it down
to get inside
even when it's coming down
the way
still knows the way . . .
So fly . . .

—Lyrics to "In the Sun" by SriMati

Field Herb Minestrone 2.0
page 270

6

SALADS
AND SOUPS

RADICCHIO, ARTICHOKE, AND HEIRLOOM TOMATO SALAD

TUSCAN KALE SALAD

TREE OF LIFE SALAD

ESCAROLE SALAD

FIELD SALAD WITH CREAMY ARTICHOKE RANCH

BALSAMIC BLACKBERRY KALE SALAD

WILD ARUGULA HEIRLOOM SALAD WITH FRESH BURRATA

PANZANELLA

"ITALIAN-ISH" MULTI-GREEN CAESAR
WITH AVOCADO BALSAMIC DRESSING AND ALMOND RICOTTA

TOMATO ENDIVE SALAD

WHITE BEAN TOMATO SOUP

FIELD HERB MINESTRONE 2.0

RADICCHIO, ARTICHOKE, AND HEIRLOOM TOMATO SALAD

SERVES 6 Radicchio comes in many different varieties. We grow a green variety in our garden at JAI. One of the best ways to eat radicchio is to grill it. I love to eat it with generous amounts of olive oil, balsamic or apple cider vinegar, sea salt, and freshly cracked black pepper. In this dish, tossing grilled radicchio with heirloom tomatoes, artichokes, and basil brings flavors that contrast its bitter taste.

INGREDIENTI

¼ cup olive oil

¼ cup balsamic or apple cider vinegar

2 teaspoons Celtic sea salt, plus more to taste

½ teaspoon freshly cracked black pepper

3 heads of radicchio, halved

4 heirloom tomatoes, sliced into quarters

1 cup artichoke hearts in a jar

Juice of 1 lemon

1 bunch fresh basil, finely sliced

PREPARAZIONE

1   In a medium shallow serving dish, whisk together 2 tablespoons olive oil, the vinegar, salt, and pepper. Set aside.

2   With metal tongs, hold each radicchio half over an open flame or place it on a gas grill barbecue. Grill it for about 5 minutes, until the leaves blacken around the edges and the colors brighten. Remove from the heat and place in the dressing, turning it over to coat the radicchio well.

3   In a small bowl, place the tomatoes and the artichoke hearts and toss well in the remaining 2 tablespoons of olive oil, the lemon juice, and salt to taste.

4   On individual plates, arrange a radicchio half in the center. Add the tomato mixture on top and garnish with fresh basil. Pour some of the remaining marinade over the radicchio.

TUSCAN KALE SALAD

SERVES 6 Every plant-based collection of recipes features one of my favorite greens: kale. Kale comes in many varieties, and there is so much to experience within the world of this vitamin K treasure. I like the curly kales for this dish because their leaves hold the dressing so beautifully. The combination of miso paste and balsamic vinegar creates an unexpected, lively flavor. Massage the dressing into the kale leaves first. Then add the other ingredients and toss to coat. I prefer to cook the beets and roast the almonds and fennel for this recipe, but, of course, you can skip these steps if you prefer an entirely raw salad.

INGREDIENTI

1 cup fresh fennel, sliced

1 cup toasted almonds

1/4 cup miso paste

1/4 cup balsamic vinegar

2 tablespoons olive oil

2 bunches fresh purple kale

4 golden beets

Fennel top, for garnish

PREPARAZIONE

1   If you'd like to roast the fennel and almonds for the salad, preheat the oven to 425 degrees F.

2   **To make the dressing:** In a small bowl, combine the miso paste, vinegar, and olive oil. Whisk together.

3   Wash the kale and strip the leaves from the stalk. Tear the leaves into 2-inch pieces, allowing for the natural variation of the leaves.

4   In a large serving bowl, place the kale and the dressing and massage the dressing into the kale. This helps soften the kale, but as you do this step, do it intentionally while thinking about the people you love and the healing power of your food. (Yes, thoughts are things and thus become important ingredients in your dish.)

5   If you like your beets raw, you can simply grate them with the skins on. Or, to cook them, bring a medium pot of water to a boil over high heat and add the beets. Cook them for about 30 minutes, until they are tender. Drain the beets in a colander and, with cool water running over them, rub the skins off with your thumbs until you have a smoothly peeled beet that is ready to be sliced. Slice the beets into $\frac{1}{8}$-inch-thick slices. Add the beets to the kale and toss to combine.

6   Spread out the fennel slices and the almonds on a rimmed baking sheet. Roast for about 8 minutes, until browned.

7   Add the almonds and fennel to the kale in the serving bowl and toss to combine.

TREE OF LIFE SALAD

SERVES 4 Red bell peppers are packed with vitamin C. I love pairing these little healers with a living green. Using watercress with its roots still intact brings the vibrancy sky high. After we've finished this salad, I plant the base and roots in my garden.

INGREDIENTI

½ cup pine nuts (pignoli)

1 bunch of living watercress or other living greens

Roasted Red Peppers (page 130)

1 small red onion, sliced

2 tablespoons extra-virgin olive oil

2 tablespoons balsamic vinegar

1 teaspoon Celtic sea salt

Freshly cracked black pepper to taste

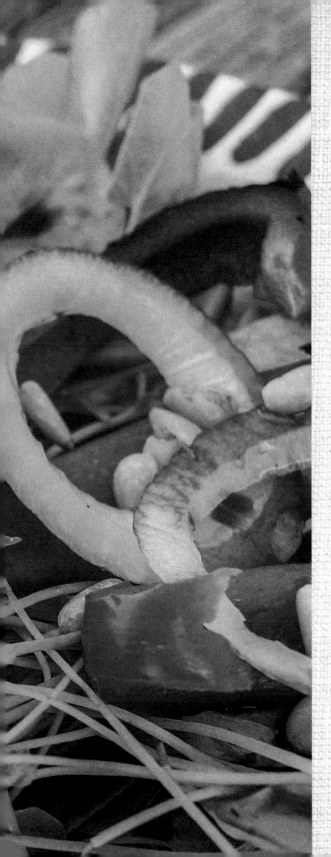

PREPARAZIONE

1 Place the pine nuts in a small pan over medium-low heat. Shake the pan to keep the pine nuts toasting on all sides (watch closely—they can burn quickly). Remove the pan from the heat when the pine nuts begin to brown and become fragrant.

2 On a serving plate, arrange the watercress and fan it out to make it look like a tree. Arrange the red bell peppers and the onion rings. Sprinkle with the pine nuts and drizzle with the olive oil and vinegar.

3 Sprinkle with salt and pepper.

ESCAROLE SALAD

SERVES 6 This hearty leaf can take the heat. I love it on a hot summer day with a generous dose of apple cider vinegar and salt to cut the bitter escarole taste. The greens will stay crispy and crunchy for hours. This simple combination is one that you'll crave—there is no salad quite like it.

INGREDIENTI

1 large head of escarole

2 tablespoons olive oil

3 to 5 tablespoons apple cider vinegar or to taste

½ to 1 teaspoon Celtic sea salt

1 cup large capers

1 cup chopped fresh flat-leaf parsley

Freshly cracked black pepper to taste

PREPARAZIONE

1   On a cutting board, slice off the base of the escarole to release the leaves.

2   In a large salad bowl, arrange the escarole leaves in whole pieces to form a fountain of greens.

3   Drizzle with olive oil and vinegar and add the salt.

4   Add the capers and parsley and toss with your hands. Finish with pepper to taste.

FIELD SALAD WITH CREAMY ARTICHOKE RANCH

SERVES 4 A fresh country salad with the power of probiotics. Choose a locally grown salad mix if you can!

INGREDIENTI

Dressing:

1 cup canned artichokes in water, drained

¼ cup olive oil

2 tablespoons nutritional yeast

Juice of ½ lemon

1 teaspoon Himalayan salt

Salad:

4 cups fresh herbed salad mix with edible flowers

1 cup Classic Fermented Garlic Kraut (page 122)

1 cup whole Italian pepperoncini from a jar, drained

Freshly cracked black pepper to taste

PREPARAZIONE

1   **To make the dressing:** In the bowl of a food processor, place the artichokes, olive oil, nutritional yeast, lemon juice, and salt. Process until smooth and creamy.

2   **To make the salad:** Arrange the salad mix in a beautiful bowl. Add the salad dressing and toss to coat. Top with dollops of sauerkraut alternating with pepperoncini.

3   Add pepper to taste.

BALSAMIC BLACKBERRY KALE SALAD

SERVES 4 This monochromatic, gorgeous purple salad is a creative and delicious summer treat. Using one pan makes for easy cleanup.

INGREDIENTI

1 tablespoon coconut oil

1 bunch of purple kale, stems removed and leaves torn into strips

1 cup raw pistachios

1 pint fresh blackberries

¼ cup balsamic vinegar

15 fresh mint leaves, for garnish

1 teaspoon Himalayan salt, for garnish

PREPARAZIONE

1   Heat the coconut oil in a cast-iron skillet over high heat. Add the kale and sauté for 2 to 4 minutes, until wilted and slightly charred. Transfer to a serving plate.

2   In the same skillet, add the pistachios and sauté them for 5 to 7 minutes, until slightly blackened.

3   Remove the pistachios from the heat and sprinkle them over the kale.

4   In the same pan, add the blackberries and vinegar. Sauté for 3 to 5minutes, until the vinegar evaporates.

5   Add the berries to the kale.

6   Garnish with the mint leaves and salt.

WILD ARUGULA HEIRLOOM SALAD WITH FRESH BURRATA

SERVES 4 TO 6 The naturally spicy flavor of the wild arugula in this salad is a perfect contrast to the creamy, full-bodied burrata.

INGREDIENTI

4 cups wild arugula

2 medium heirloom tomatoes, sliced into 3/8-inch-thick slices

1 cup field greens and edible flowers mix

6 slices Macadamia Cashew Burrata (page 60)

2 tablespoons balsamic vinegar

2 tablespoons olive oil

1 teaspoon Celtic salt

1/2 teaspoon freshly cracked black pepper

PREPARAZIONE

1   Arrange the arugula in a ring along the outer edge of a flat, round serving dish.

2   Make a ring of tomato slices inside the arugula ring.

3   Place a handful of the greens in the center of the tomato ring.

4   Place the burrata slices on top of the tomatoes to make a flower design. Drizzle with balsamic vinegar and olive oil. Season with the salt and pepper.

PANZANELLA

SERVES 4 A wonderful way to showcase heirloom tomatoes, this recipe is a traditional Tuscan favorite. You can keep it high vibe by using a fermented sourdough baguette.

INGREDIENTI

¾ cup olive oil

1 small shallot, thinly sliced

2 garlic cloves, pressed

6 ripe, succulent heirloom tomatoes, sliced into wedges

1 teaspoon large-grain Celtic sea salt

One 2-day-old baguette broken into 1- to 2-inch pieces

1 large bunch of fresh basil

Juice of 1 lemon

Freshly ground black pepper to taste

PREPARAZIONE

1   In a serving bowl, place the olive oil, shallot, and garlic.

2   Add the tomato wedges.

3   Add the salt and stir to coat.

4   Fold the bread pieces into the marinade so that they soak in the juices.

5   Slice the basil into thin ribbons, reserving some leaves for garnish. Add to the salad.

6   Squeeze the lemon juice over the mixture and finish with pepper. Garnish with the reserved basil.

"ITALIAN-ISH" MULTI-GREEN CAESAR WITH AVOCADO BALSAMIC DRESSING AND ALMOND RICOTTA

SERVES 6 I read recently that Caesar salad may have been invented by an Italian who made his way to Mexico. That made me question whether this Caesar recipe fit in this book at all. But in the end, the lively, creamy taste of this salad won me over. I'm sure it will win you over too. Let's just call it "Italian-ish."

Salad:	Avocado Balsamic Caesar Dressing:
2 cups fresh spinach	1 avocado, halved and pitted
2 cups romaine	1 tablespoon balsamic vinegar
2 cups baby kale	2 tablespoons nutritional yeast
2 cups grapes, halved	Juice of 1/2 lemon
6 local passion fruit, halved (optional)	1 teaspoon Worcestershire sauce
1 cup fresh Cashew Almond Ricotta (page 68)	1 teaspoon Celtic sea salt
	Freshly cracked black pepper to taste

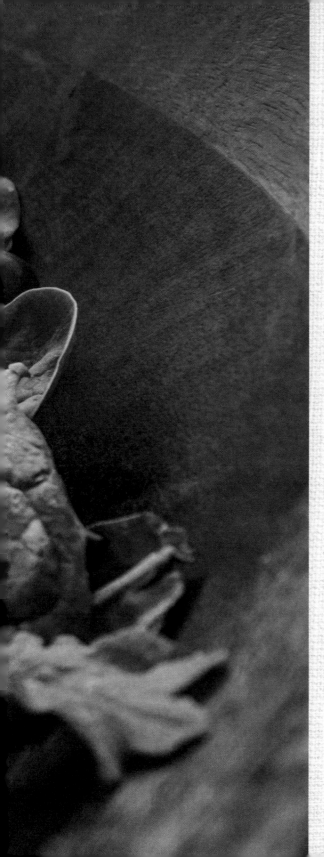

1 **To make the salad:** In a large wooden salad bowl, layer the spinach, romaine, and kale.

2 **To make the dressing:** In the bowl of a food processor or high-speed blender, place the avocado, vinegar, nutritional yeast, lemon juice, Worcestershire, salt, pepper, and ½ cup of water. Blend on medium speed for about 30 seconds, until well combined.

3 Massage the dressing into the greens using your hands and loving thoughts.

4 **To complete the salad:** Sprinkle the grape halves on top of the greens and add the passion fruit, if using.

5 Top with tablespoons of Cashew Almond Ricotta.

6 Garnish with pepper.

TOMATO ENDIVE SALAD

SERVES 4 A salad featuring whole foods from the Italian countryside. It's a welcome companion to hearty pastas and lasagnas. Its beauty is in its simplicity.

INGREDIENTI

2 tablespoons balsamic vinegar

1 tablespoon organic sugar

2 pints cherry tomatoes, stems removed, sliced in half

2 endives, finely sliced

1 teaspoon Celtic sea salt

2 tablespoons extra-virgin olive oil

PREPARAZIONE

1   In a small saucepan over low heat, add the vinegar and sugar and reduce, stirring constantly for 8 minutes, until it coats the back of a spoon.

2   Place the tomatoes and endives in a beautiful serving bowl.

3   Pour the balsamic reduction over the tomatoes and endives and season with salt and olive oil.

WHITE BEAN TOMATO SOUP

SERVES 6 My favorite soup at Iesolana, this protein-rich bowl is so satisfying that you will want a second helping. It's wonderful served with fresh-baked rustic bread.

INGREDIENTI

4 tablespoons extra-virgin olive oil

5 garlic cloves, sliced

2 tablespoons chopped fresh sage

Two 15-ounce cans of Italian white beans in liquid

2 cups Mathis's Simply Red Tomato Sauce (page 44)

1 tablespoon Celtic sea salt

Freshly cracked black pepper to taste

1 In a large saucepan over medium heat, warm
   3 tablespoons of the extra-virgin olive oil,
   then add the garlic and sauté until the aroma
   releases. Add in the sage and stir to coat. Add
   the white beans plus liquid and combine with
   the sage and garlic. Simmer on low heat for
   8 minutes, until heated through.

2 Add the tomato sauce and salt and let cook
   for another 8 minutes or more.

3 Drizzle with the remaining 1 tablespoon olive
   oil and season with salt and pepper.

FIELD HERB MINESTRONE 2.0

SERVES 2 TO 4 This aromatic veggie stew is a greener, more vibrant version of the original classic. Feel free to add more of the alkalizing apple cider vinegar and mineral sea salt to taste.

INGREDIENTI

Half of a 6-ounce package organic pasta

1 pint cherry tomatoes, stems removed

2 celery stalks, coarsely chopped

4 multicolored carrots, coarsely chopped

One 6-ounce can of tomato paste

One 15.5-ounce can of kidney beans, drained

2 tablespoons fresh dill

2 tablespoons fresh parsley

2 teaspoons fresh oregano

1 leaf purple kale, coarsely chopped

1 large leaf Swiss chard, coarsely chopped

2 teaspoons Celtic sea salt

Freshly cracked black pepper to taste

2 tablespoons apple cider vinegar

Juice of ½ lemon

1 bunch broccoli sprouts, for garnish

Edible flowers, for garnish

PREPARAZIONE

1. Prepare the pasta according to the package directions. Drain the pasta and set aside.

2. Heat a cast-iron wok or deep saucepan over high heat and add the tomatoes. Cook until blackened (no need for oil). Reduce the heat to medium.

3. Add the celery to the pan and stir for about 3 minutes, until its color brightens.

4. Add the carrots and sauté for 3 minutes.

5. In the bowl of a high-speed blender, process the tomato paste and 2 cups filtered water until smooth. Pour into the pan with the tomatoes, celery, and carrots. Reduce the heat to low and simmer for 5 minutes.

6. Add the kidney beans and the pasta. Then add the dill, parsley, and oregano. Stir to combine.

7. Gently fold the kale and Swiss chard into the soup. Add the salt, pepper, vinegar, and lemon juice. Adjust the seasonings to taste.

8. Garnish with broccoli sprouts and edible flowers.

COMMUNITY

Beyond race, creed, gender, ideology, religion, political party, or sexual preference, we are Earthlings. We are intricately connected to this planet we are riding on. We are the global Citizens of Planet Earth.

Our collective decisions around lifestyle and consumption have caused the temperature levels of the planet to rise to unprecedented levels. Global warming is currently over 400 percent in excess of temperatures ever experienced on this planet. Unchecked, this heat will continue to have increasingly devastating effects upon all life on Earth.

Fortunately, there are many things we can do to draw down this heat. Activist and author Paul Hawken, along with a coalition of scientists, activists, and policy makers, has created a strategy of 100 solutions to reverse global warming. Project Drawdown is a comprehensive strategy that includes actionable solutions we can all take part in right now.

Number 4 on the list of the hundred most powerful things you can do to reverse global warming is eating a plant-rich diet.

"If cattle were a nation, they would be the world's third-largest emitter of greenhouse gases." —Paul Hawken

Like Paul, we believe in the great empathy, compassion, and intelligence of humanity to take responsibility for global warming, to commit to making the necessary changes to draw down the heat and preserve life on our sacred planet.

You can make a powerful difference to draw down global warming at each meal by choosing plants on your plate. When you choose to eat plant-rich, you will save thousands of gallons of water, acres of sacred lands, and our precious magnificent trees, which are the very lungs of our planet. And by choosing plants, you'll experience greater compassion by saving one animal's life. That is powerful change you can make today!

There is no time like the present. We believe in you. We are the ones we've been waiting for.

Eat plants!

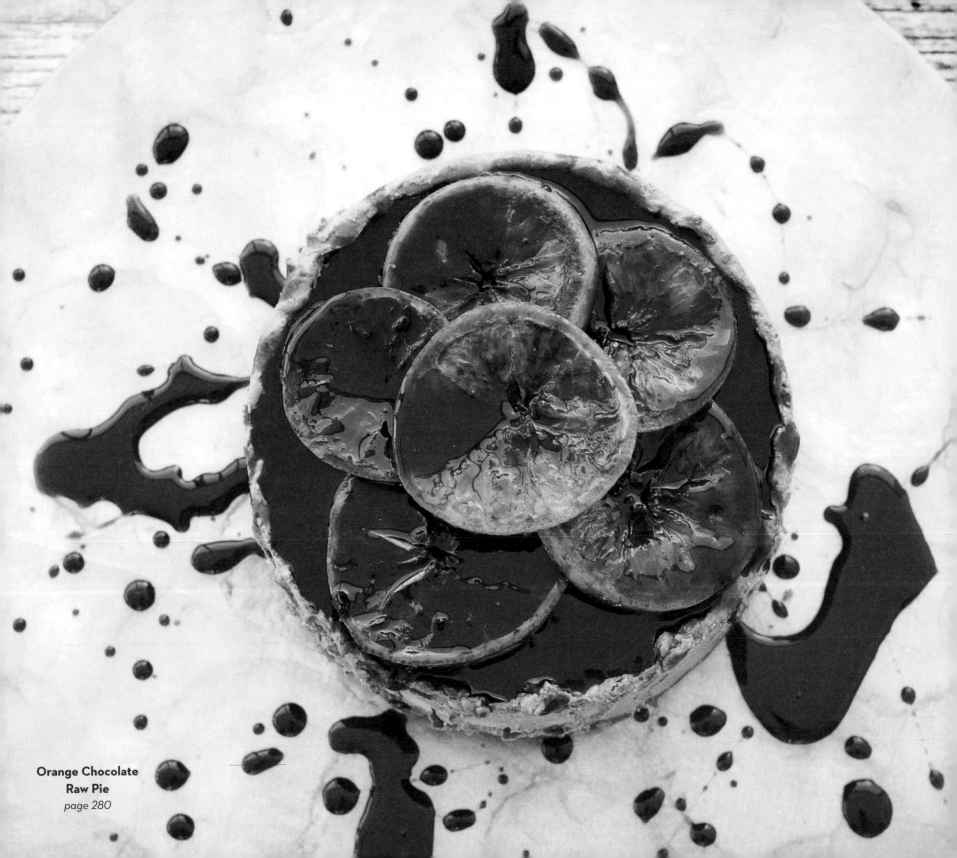

**Orange Chocolate
Raw Pie**
page 280

7

DESSERTS

BLACKBERRY BALSAMIC LEMON TART

ORANGE CHOCOLATE RAW PIE

POACHED PEAR TART

CHOCOLATE SALAMI

ESPRESSO ICE CREAM

BLUEBERRY CASHEW GELATO

PISTACHIO GELATO

CREAMY LEMON GELATO

PEAR GRANITA

GLUTEN-FREE AND DAIRY-FREE TIRAMISU

MASCARPONE CHEESE

COUNTRY-STYLE CACAO MOUSSE

ARBORIO RICE PUDDING

BLACKBERRY TRIFLE WITH COCONUT CASHEW CREAM

LAVENDER CHEESECAKE

CARAMEL BRÛLÉE

POACHED PEARS WITH ALMOND HONEY CREAM

POACHED NECTARINES

TAMARA'S ALMOND CAKE

ALMOND MERINGUE COOKIES

EASY ALMOND ORANGE COOKIES

JUPITER GRAPE CAKE

BLACKBERRY BALSAMIC LEMON TART

SERVES 6 This combination of flavors creates the perfect warm berry tart. You can adjust the sugar quantity based on the ripeness of your blackberries and your own taste. Blackberries are very high in antioxidants, so consider adding them into your dishes whenever possible.

INGREDIENTI

6 Medjool or specialty dates

Coconut oil, for greasing the tart pan

2 cups raw almonds

1/4 cup uncooked oatmeal

1/2 teaspoon Celtic sea salt

Zest of 1 lemon

4 pints fresh blackberries (local if possible)

1/2 cup balsamic vinegar

1/2 cup sugar

5 large fresh basil leaves, sliced thinly, for garnish

IN ANTICIPO:

Place the dates in filtered water in a small bowl and soak for 30 minutes. Drain the dates and remove the pits.

PREPARAZIONE

1 Preheat the oven to 350 degrees F. Lightly grease the sides and bottom of a 9 x 9-inch tart pan with coconut oil.

2 In the bowl of a food processor, place the almonds and pulse until mealy in texture. Add the oatmeal and salt and pulse a few more times.

3 With the motor running, add one date at a time until a ball forms on the side of the bowl.

4 Press the crust mixture into the prepared tart pan and flatten it with the palms of your hands.

5 Top the crust mixture with the lemon zest, distributing it as evenly as possible.

6 Arrange the blackberries in rows on the surface of the crust. Bake for 30 minutes.

7 In a small saucepan over medium heat, place the vinegar and sugar. Stir until the sugar dissolves and the mixture turns into a glaze. Remove the tart from the oven and drizzle lightly with the balsamic glaze.

8 Garnish with the sliced basil.

ORANGE CHOCOLATE RAW PIE

SERVES 8 A work of art, this pie is both gorgeous and delicious. It is also deceptively easy. Once you get the hang of it, there is no end to the flavors you can create. Use a 6-inch springform pan for the full effect. Don't be shy with the glaze. Go for it! Remember, you're creating food as art.

INGREDIENTI

Crust:

18 Medjool dates

1 teaspoon coconut oil, for greasing the pan

3 cups raw walnuts

1/2 teaspoon Himalayan salt

1 tablespoon orange zest

Filling:

4 cups raw cashews

One 15-ounce can of coconut milk

1/4 cup cacao butter

5 tablespoons raw cacao powder

1 teaspoon orange zest

Balsamic Glaze:

1/2 cup balsamic vinegar

1/2 cup sugar

1 orange, sliced thinly, for garnish

1. **Place the dates in filtered water in a small bowl. Cover and refrigerate overnight.**

2. **Place the cashews in filtered water in a small bowl. Cover and refrigerate overnight.**

PREPARAZIONE

1   **To make the crust:** Lightly oil a 6-inch springform pan with coconut oil.

2   In the bowl of a food processor, place the walnuts and pulse until mealy.

3   Drain the water from the dates. Remove and compost the pits.

4   With the motor running, add 8 to 10 of the pitted dates to the bowl of the food processor one at a time and blend until the dough balls up on the side of the bowl.

5   Press the dough into the bottom of the prepared springform pan in an even layer to form the crust of the pie. Sprinkle the top of the crust evenly with the salt and orange zest.

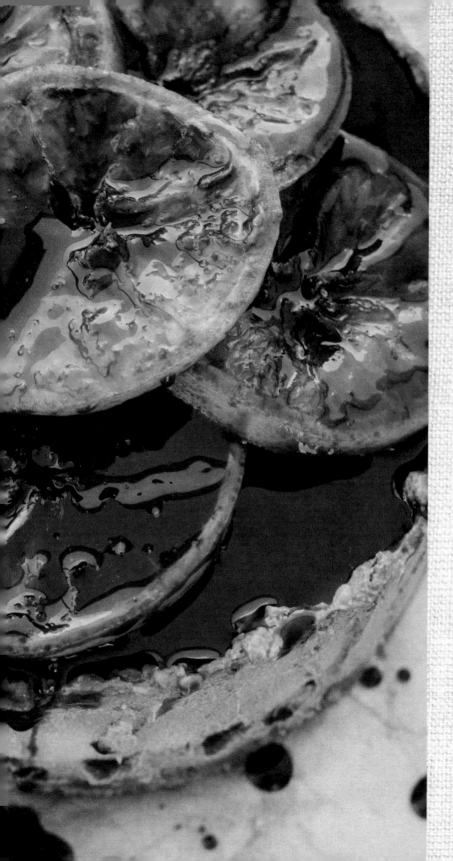

6   **To make the filling:** Drain the cashews.

7   In the bowl of a Vitamix or high-speed blender, place the cashews, coconut milk, cacao butter, the remaining dates, the cacao powder, and orange zest. Blend on medium speed for 30 seconds, then increase to high speed and blend for 1 minute more or until the filling is silky smooth.

8   Pour the filling into the crust and smooth it with a rubber spatula. Transfer the pie to the freezer overnight.

The day of serving:

9   **To make the balsamic glaze:** Place the vinegar in a large saucepan over medium heat and add the sugar. Stir until the sugar is dissolved. Continue stirring the mixture as it cooks for about 8 minutes, until it reduces down to a glaze.

10   Remove the pie from the freezer and let it stand for 30 minutes before serving. Using a butter knife, loosen the pie from the sides of the pan with an up-and-down motion. This will create the pretty vertical texture on the sides of the pie. (I know. Happy accident.)

11   Garnish with the orange slices and drizzle with balsamic glaze.

POACHED PEAR TART

SERVES 8 This dessert is a rustic preparation that showcases the whole fruit. I leave the skins on and poach the pears ahead of time, which makes the preparation super easy. The raw crust is a beautiful contrast to the warm, full-bodied pears, and the dark, glossy balsamic reduction gives it an Italian flair in both taste and fashion. The perfect finish to any Italian meal, this tart is considerably low in sugar, as the bulk of the sugar content reduces in the glaze. The sweetness comes mostly from the pears themselves and the dates in the crust.

INGREDIENTI

Filling:

2 teaspoons coconut oil, for greasing the pans and baking sheet

6 organic red local pears

Crust:

2 cups almonds

10 Medjool dates

1/2 teaspoon Celtic sea salt

Balsamic Glaze:

1/4 cup balsamic vinegar

1 cup raw turbinado sugar

1. **Rinse the almonds well. Place them in filtered water in a small bowl. Cover and refrigerate overnight.**
2. **Soak the dates in filtered water in a small bowl for 30 minutes. Drain the dates, remove the pits, and set aside.**

PREPARAZIONE

1   **To make the filling:** Preheat the oven to 350 degrees F.

2   Grease a rimmed baking sheet with coconut oil.

3   Halve and core the pears, leaving the skins on.

4   Place the pears flesh-side down on the prepared baking sheet and bake for about 8 minutes.

5   Pour 1/4 cup water into the bottom of the baking sheet and continue to poach the pears for 8 minutes more.

6   **To make the crust:** Drain the almonds.

7   In the bowl of a food processor, pulse the almonds until mealy. With the motor running, add the soaked and pitted dates one at a time until the mixture balls up on one side of the bowl.

8   Lightly oil a 9-inch round tart pan. Press the crust evenly into the pan and sprinkle it with salt.

9   On a cutting board, using a sharp knife, slice the pears into 2-inch-thick slices, leaving the skins on.

10   Arrange the pears in a circular pattern, slightly overlapping, from the outside edge to the inside center, until you have a pretty mandala or flower pattern.

11   **To make the balsamic glaze:** In a small saucepan over low heat, combine the vinegar and sugar and reduce, stirring constantly for 8 minutes, until it coats the back of a spoon.

12   Drizzle the balsamic glaze in a pretty pattern over the pears. Serve!

CHOCOLATE SALAMI

SERVES 8 Taking superfood cacao to the next level, this recipe is certainly the healthiest salami you will ever eat. Free of the eggs and butter characteristic of this traditional Italian dessert, this salami is a vital energy booster. Bursting with decadent flavors, it is la dolce vita.

INGREDIENTI

4 Medjool dates

5 dried apricots

2 cups raw walnuts

¼ teaspoon Celtic
sea salt

½ cup hardened
coconut butter

3 tablespoons raw
cacao powder

1 cup raw pistachios

2 tablespoons espresso

IN ANTICIPO:

Place the dates and apricots in filtered water in a small
bowl and soak for 1 hour. Drain the dates and apricots,
then remove the pits from the dates and apricots. Set aside.

PREPARAZIONE

1   In the bowl of a food processor, place the walnuts and salt and pulse until the mixture is mealy in texture.

2   Add the coconut butter and cacao powder and pulse until well incorporated.

3   Add ¾ cup of the pistachios and pulse about six times, until the nuts are broken into pea-size pieces. Ideally, you want to have a few larger pieces too, so they are visible when you slice the salami.

4   With the motor running, add the espresso. Drop the pitted apricots and the pitted dates into the mixture one at a time until a ball forms on the side of the bowl.

5   Remove the mixture and place it on wax paper. Using the paper, roll the dough back and forth to form a cylindrical salami. If it gets sticky, lightly grease your hands with a bit of coconut oil. Wrap the salami in foil and refrigerate it for 3 hours or until firm.

6   Place the salami on a cutting board. Chop the remaining ¼ cup of pistachios coarsely and press them into the top of the salami.

ESPRESSO
ICE CREAM

SERVES 2 TO 4 Although I am not a fan of morning coffee, I happen to adore coffee-flavored ice cream. This espresso ice cream perfectly re-creates the aroma of Italy. Of course, it's superior if you use an ice-cream maker, but I found that you can get away with a metal pan and a food processor.

INGREDIENTI

5 Medjool dates

6 tablespoons fresh-pressed
strong espresso

Two 15-ounce cans of refrigerated
whole coconut milk

2 teaspoons almond extract

2 tablespoons grated raw cacao
or dark chocolate, for garnish

IN ANTICIPO:

**Place the dates in filtered water in a small bowl
and soak for at least 30 minutes.
Drain the dates and remove the pits.**

PREPARAZIONE

1 Prepare the espresso in a French press or espresso maker. Set aside.

2 Open the cans of coconut milk and scoop out the solidified coconut milk, reserving the liquid.

3 In the pitcher of a Vitamix or high-speed blender, add the solidified coconut milk, the soaked and pitted dates, the almond extract, and ¼ cup of the espresso. Blend on medium speed while adding small amounts of the reserved coconut milk liquid 2 tablespoons at a time until the mixture is smooth and thick.

4 Prepare the ice cream in an ice-cream maker following the manufacturer's instructions. Alternately, pour the ice-cream mixture into a metal loaf pan and cover it with parchment paper. Freeze until hardened.

5   Remove the pan from the freezer to thaw. As the mixture gets loosened a bit, use a knife to break it up and place it in the bowl of a food processor to blend again. This second step gives the ice cream a creamier texture.

6   Return the ice cream to freeze one more time, for at least 3 hours. Remove from the freezer 15 minutes before serving.

7   Scoop the ice cream into a shallow bowl. Pour the remaining 2 tablespoons of espresso over the top. Garnish with shavings of raw cacao.

BLUEBERRY CASHEW GELATO

SERVES 2 TO 4 This creamy gelato is bursting with healing indigo hues. It is a perfect summertime treat.

INGREDIENTI

1 cup cashews	1 tablespoon refined coconut oil
¾ pint fresh blueberries, plus more for garnish	
	1 teaspoon lemon zest
1 cup full-fat coconut milk	¼ cup agave
½ cup cocoa butter	Pinch of salt

IN ANTICIPO:

Place the cashews in filtered water in a small bowl.
Cover and refrigerate overnight.

PREPARAZIONE

1   Drain the cashews.

2   In the bowl of a Vitamix or high-speed blender, place the drained cashews, 1 cup of the blueberries, the coconut milk, cocoa butter, coconut oil, lemon zest, agave, and salt, and blend on medium speed until smooth.

3   Transfer the mixture to a metal loaf pan, even out the top, and gently press the remaining ½ cup of blueberries onto the surface.

4   Cover the pan with parchment paper and place it in the freezer for a minimum of 8 hours.

5   Thaw for approximately 30 minutes before serving.

6   Using an ice-cream scoop, transfer the gelato to a small serving bowl. Garnish with more fresh blueberries.

PISTACHIO GELATO

SERVES 2 TO 4 One of my all-time favorites, the pistachio flavor in this delicious gelato brings Italy home.

INGREDIENTI

1¼ cups raw whole pistachios, plus more for garnish

2 tablespoons refined coconut oil

½ cup cocoa butter

½ cup light agave

1 cup full-fat coconut milk

**Place the pistachios in filtered water in a small bowl.
Cover and refrigerate overnight.**

PREPARAZIONE

1   Drain the pistachios.

2   In the bowl of a Vitamix or high-speed blender, place 1 cup of the pistachios, the coconut oil, the cacao butter, agave, and coconut milk and blend on medium speed until smooth.

3   Transfer the mixture to a metal loaf pan, even out the top with a rubber spatula, and sprinkle the remaining ¼ cup of pistachios over the top.

4   Cover with parchment paper and place in the freezer for a minimum of 8 hours.

5   Thaw for 15 minutes before serving.

6   Using an ice-cream scoop, create a tower with three scoops. Garnish with more pistachios.

CREAMY LEMON GELATO

SERVES 2 TO 4 Light, tart, and sweet, this creamy dessert is the perfect finish to any hearty Italian meal.

INGREDIENTI

1 cup cashews

1 large lemon, peeled and seeded

1 cup coconut water

1 cup organic sugar

1 tablespoon lemon zest, for garnish

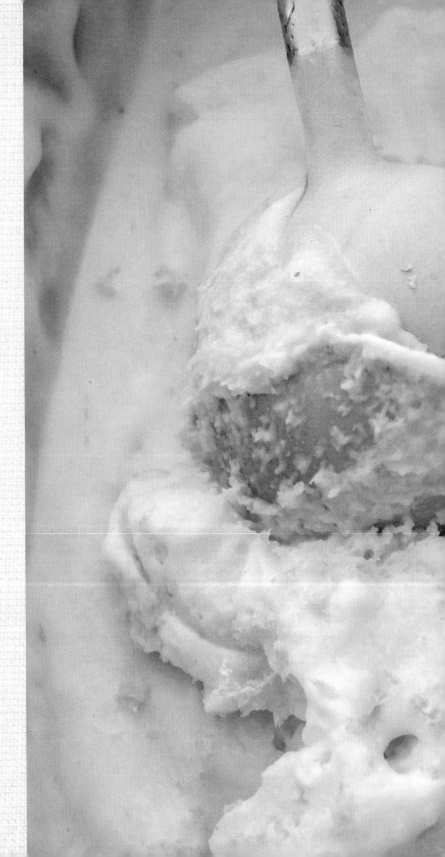

IN ANTICIPO:
Place the cashews in filtered water in a small bowl.
Cover and refrigerate overnight.

PREPARAZIONE

1 Drain the cashews.

2 In the bowl of a Vitamix or high-speed blender, place the cashews, lemon, coconut water, and sugar and blend on medium speed until smooth.

3 Transfer to a metal loaf pan and even out the top using a rubber spatula.

4 Cover with parchment paper and place in the freezer for a minimum of 8 hours.

5 Thaw 15 minutes before serving. Using an ice-cream scoop, transfer the gelato to a serving bowl. Garnish with lemon zest.

PEAR GRANITA

SERVES 2 This is an easy take on shaved ice. If you juice the fruit yourself, it will enhance the taste dramatically. Granita has an icy texture that is delightfully refreshing after a delicious Italian meal. I hope this recipe inspires you to try out many flavors. I also love using melon, as well as lemon garnished with basil.

INGREDIENTI

4 cups high-quality pear juice

4 tablespoons maple syrup (optional)

1 teaspoon ground cinnamon, plus more for garnish

PREPARAZIONE

1   In the bowl of a Vitamix or high-speed blender, add the pear juice, maple syrup if using, and cinnamon and blend on medium speed until well incorporated.

2   Pour the mixture into a metal loaf pan, cover with parchment paper, and freeze for 8 hours or until hardened.

3   Using a metal ice-cream scoop, shave off the top layer of the frozen granita and add it to a small glass. Finish by pressing the granita at the top so that it forms a mound. Garnish the granita with a bit of ground cinnamon.

GLUTEN-FREE AND DAIRY-FREE TIRAMISU

SERVES 8 All the taste and texture of a traditional tiramisu without the complicated layering. I created this recipe so you can bake the cake right in the pan and then add layers of mascarpone and mousse on top. I prefer a denser cake than the sponge variety called for in proper Italian recipes. Aquafaba is the secret ingredient in this recipe—it's used in all the layers. It takes quite a while for the peaks to form, sometimes as long as 15 minutes. But don't give up! Keep at it and you will discover a meringue so glossy and delicious, you won't believe this dessert is vegan and dairy-free.

INGREDIENTI

Refined coconut oil, for greasing the pan

2 cups Almond Milk (page 22)

2 teaspoons apple cider vinegar

¾ cup aquafaba (liquid from canned garbanzo beans)

1½ cups superfine sugar (finely granulated white sugar) or powdered sugar

¼ teaspoon cream of tartar

2 cups organic white baking flour

1 teaspoon baking soda

1 teaspoon baking powder

½ teaspoon fine sea salt

1 cup strong espresso

2 cups Mascarpone Cheese (page 306)

2 cups Country-Style Cacao Mousse (page 308)

⅛ cup raw cacao powder

IN ANTICIPO:

**Chill the aquafaba for at least
30 minutes before whipping.**

PREPARAZIONE

1   Preheat the oven to 350 degrees F. Grease a
9 x 13-inch pan with refined coconut oil.

2   Place the almond milk in a small bowl and add
the vinegar. Set aside.

3   In the bowl of an electric mixer, whip the
aquafaba on high for 8 minutes, until it
becomes milky. Add the sugar and cream of
tartar and continue whipping for 8 minutes
more, until the mixture is glossy and stiff
peaks form.

4   In a medium bowl, sift together the flour,
baking soda, baking powder, and salt.

5   Create a well in the middle of the dry
ingredients. Pour in the almond milk–vinegar
mixture and mix well.

6   Fold in the aquafaba-sugar mixture until incorporated.

7   Transfer the batter to the prepared pan and shake slightly to even it out.

8   Bake for 30 minutes or until a fork inserted in the center comes out clean.

9   Remove the cake from the oven and let it cool in the pan. When the cake has cooled, pour the espresso over the cake, letting it soak in well.

10   Fold the mascarpone into the center of the cake. Using a rubber spatula, carefully spread it to the outer edges in an even layer. Chill for 3 hours or more.

11   Fold the chocolate mousse into the center of the chilled cake. Using a rubber spatula, spread the mousse to the outer edges of the pan.

12   Sift the raw cacao powder over the top of the cake. Chill for at least 3 hours more.

13   Cut the servings right out of the pan and serve!

MASCARPONE CHEESE

MAKES ABOUT 2 CUPS Mascarpone cheese is used in many classic tiramisu recipes. This one is dairy-free. You can use blanched almonds or pine nuts as substitutes for the cashews.

INGREDIENTI

2 cups cashews

½ cup aquafaba (liquid from canned garbanzo beans)

1 cup superfine sugar (finely granulated white sugar) or powdered sugar

¼ teaspoon cream of tartar

Juice of 2 lemons

IN ANTICIPO:

1. Place the cashews in filtered water in a small bowl. Cover and refrigerate overnight.
2. Chill the aquafaba for at least 30 minutes before whipping.

PREPARAZIONE

1   Drain the cashews.

2   In the bowl of an electric mixer, whip the aquafaba on high for 8 minutes or until it gets milky. Add the sugar and cream of tartar. Continue whipping for about 8 minutes more, until the mixture is glossy and stiff peaks form.

3   In the bowl of a Vitamix or high-speed blender, place the cashews, lemon juice, and aquafaba mixture. Blend on medium speed until smooth.

4   Spread on crackers or use in Gluten-Free and Dairy-Free Tiramisu (page 302).

COUNTRY-STYLE CACAO MOUSSE

MAKES ABOUT 2 CUPS You will taste some textured bits of the almond meal and dates, which I love.

INGREDIENTI

8 Medjool dates

3/4 cup aquafaba (liquid from canned garbanzo beans)

1/4 teaspoon cream of tartar

1 teaspoon almond extract

1 1/2 cups powdered sugar

2 cups almond meal

1/2 cup raw cacao

1/2 cup cocoa butter

IN ANTICPO:

1. Place the dates in filtered water in a small bowl and soak for 30 minutes or more. Drain the dates and remove the pits. Set aside.

2. Chill the aquafaba for at least 30 minutes before whipping.

---

1. In a large bowl fitted with an electric mixer, whip the aquafaba on high for about 8 minutes, until it starts to get milky. Add the cream of tartar, almond extract, and sugar and continue whipping for 8 minutes more, until the mixture is glossy and stiff peaks form.

2. In the bowl of a Vitamix or high-speed blender, place the almond meal, raw cacao, cocoa butter, pitted dates, and the aquafaba mixture and blend on medium speed for about 30 seconds.

3. Spoon the mousse into serving bowls or use in Gluten-Free and Dairy-Free Tiramisu (page 302).

ARBORIO RICE PUDDING

SERVES 2 This recipe was born from having an excess of rice for a risotto I was working on. The creamy texture of Arborio rice is perfect for a rice pudding dessert. It's a great way to get two dishes from one. As you prepare your risotto rice, you can skim off a bit and set it aside to whip up this pudding.

INGREDIENTI

2 dates

1½ cups cooked Arborio rice

1 vanilla bean

1 teaspoon lemon zest

1 teaspoon cardamom

1 teaspoon honey or agave, for drizzle

Fresh lemon slices, for garnish

IN ANTICIPO:
Soak the dates in warm water for at least 30 minutes.
Drain the dates, remove the pits, and place the dates
in the bowl of a Vitamix or high-speed blender.
Blend on medium speed until smooth.

———

PREPARAZIONE

1 Fold the processed dates into the rice and
   incorporate well.

2 Split the vanilla bean lengthwise and scrape out
   the insides.

3 Add the vanilla bean, lemon zest, and
   cardamom to the rice mixture. Mix well.

4 Transfer the rice pudding to individual serving
   bowls, drizzle with honey, and garnish with a
   fresh lemon slice.

BLACKBERRY TRIFLE WITH COCONUT CASHEW CREAM

SERVES 4 Comfort steams from this warm berry bowl of sweetness. Enjoy this by the fire in the colder months of the year.

INGREDIENTI

Crust:

8 to 10 Medjool or specialty dates

2 cups raw almonds

1/2 teaspoon Celtic sea salt

Coconut oil, for greasing the casserole dish

Blackberry Compote:

1/2 cup balsamic vinegar

1 cup sugar

4 pints fresh blackberries

Cream and Garnish:

Coconut Cashew Cream (page 58)

3 fresh basil leaves, finely sliced, for garnish

IN ANTICIPO:
Place the dates in filtered water in a small bowl
and soak for 30 minutes. Drain the dates,
remove the pits, and set aside.

PREPARAZIONE

1   **To make the crust:** In the bowl of a food processor, place the almonds and pulse until mealy in texture. Add the salt and pulse a few more times.

2   With the motor running, add one date at a time until a ball forms on the side of the bowl.

3   Lightly oil the sides and bottom of a small casserole dish. Press a quarter of the crust mixture into the bottom of the prepared dish, reserving the rest to crumble among the berries.

4   **To make the blackberry compote:** In a large saucepan over medium-low heat, place the vinegar and 1/2 cup of the sugar and stir for 8 to 10 minutes, until the sugar dissolves and the mixture reduces to a glaze.

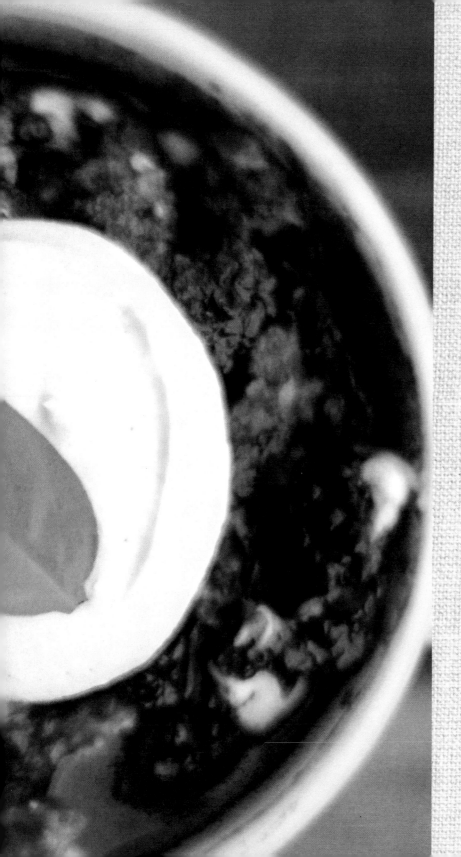

5 Add the blackberries and the remaining ½ cup of sugar to the saucepan. Continue to cook just until the berries are hot and the juices have released but they retain their shape. Be careful to not overcook them.

6 Using a slotted spoon, lift half of the berries from the juice and spoon them onto the crust in the casserole dish.

7 Spoon about 2 tablespoons of the coconut cream on top of the berries.

8 Sprinkle with the remaining crust mixture, then add more berries and top it off with a dollop of cream.

9 Garnish with the basil.

LAVENDER CHEESECAKE

SERVES 8 Special enough for a wedding in the Italian countryside, this cake is delicious and memorable. Infused with lemon, lavender, and love, you will swoon with each bite.

INGREDIENTI

Crust:

8 to 10 pitted dates

1 teaspoon coconut oil, for greasing the pan

2½ cups raw almonds

Pinch of Himalayan salt

Filling:

4 cups raw cashews

One 15-ounce can of coconut milk

2 tablespoons coconut oil

½ cup light agave

4 tablespoons fresh or dried lavender blossoms from your garden or a farmer's market, plus more for garnish

1 teaspoon freshly squeezed lemon juice

IN ANTICIPO:

1. Place the cashews in filtered water in a small bowl. Cover and refrigerate overnight.
2. Place the dates in filtered water in a small bowl and soak for 30 minutes. Drain the dates, remove the pits, and set aside.

PREPARAZIONE

1. **To make the crust:** Lightly oil a 9-inch springform pan with coconut oil.

2. In the bowl of a food processor, place the almonds and pulse until mealy in texture.

3. With the motor running, add the soaked and pitted dates one at a time until the mixture forms a ball on the side of the bowl.

4. Press the crust into the bottom of the prepared springform pan.

5. Sprinkle the crust with salt.

6   **To make the filling:** Drain the cashews.

7   In the bowl of a Vitamix or high-speed blender, place the cashews, coconut milk, coconut oil, agave, lavender flowers, and lemon juice. Blend on high speed for 3 minutes.

8   Pour the mixture over the crust. With a rubber spatula, even out the mixture using circular motions.

9   Place the pan in the freezer for 8 hours or overnight.

10   Remove the pan from the freezer and let thaw for 30 minutes before slicing. Garnish with fresh garden lavender.

CARAMEL BRÛLÉE

MAKES TWO 3-INCH RAMEKINS This decadent dessert gets its caramel flavor from Khadrawi dates. You can find them at local farmer's markets and specialty grocery stores. Mother Nature created a spectrum of dates with different flavor notes and qualities. Much like wine and chocolate, dates offer exciting culinary possibilities. I hope this recipe inspires you to explore the amazing world of this whole-food natural sweetener.

INGREDIENTI

2 cups raw whole cashews

15 Khadrawi dates

1/2 cup canned coconut milk

1/4 cup cacao butter

1/2 cup aquafaba (liquid from canned garbanzo beans)

1/4 cup organic sugar (optional)

IN ANTICIPO:

**1. Place the cashews in filtered water in a small bowl.
Cover and refrigerate overnight.
2. Place the dates in filtered water in a small bowl.
Cover and refrigerate overnight.**

PREPARAZIONE

1   Drain the cashews and the dates. Remove the pits from the dates.

2   In the bowl of a Vitamix or high-speed blender, place the cashews, 10 of the pitted dates, the coconut milk, cacao butter, and aquafaba and blend on medium speed, using the plunger to evenly distribute the mixture until smooth. Then process on high speed for 1 minute more, until silky smooth. Refrigerate for 3 hours or more.

3   Chop the remaining 5 dates into ¼-inch pieces and place them in the bottom of the ramekins.

4   Fold the mixture over the dates, filling the ramekin to the top. Smooth out with a rubber spatula.

5   Enjoy as is or sprinkle the sugar over the top and brown using a chef's torch. (Follow the manufacturer's directions for safety.)

POACHED PEARS WITH ALMOND HONEY CREAM

SERVES 2 Although this recipe calls for an entire bottle of wine, there is virtually no alcohol taste or content left after the wine reduces to a smoky, caramelized glaze. I chose to substitute almond extract to get the essence of amaretto without the alcohol. This is another recipe that showcases the whole-food aspect that I love so much about eating plant-based.

INGREDIENTI

½ cup almonds

1 bottle white organic Italian wine

1 cup sugar

4 local firm pears, any variety

1 teaspoon coconut oil

1 tablespoon raw local honey or agave

2 teaspoons almond extract or amaretto

4 tablespoons coconut water

In a small saucepan over high heat, bring 2 cups of water to a boil. Add the almonds and boil for 1 minute, then drain and rinse them in a colander. The skins should easily rub off with your fingers. Then place the skinned almonds in filtered water in a small bowl. Cover and refrigerate overnight.

PREPARAZIONE

1   In a large pot over medium heat, pour the bottle of wine and add the sugar. Heat the mixture for 5 minutes, stirring constantly, until the sugar dissolves.

2   Add the whole pears. Cover with a tight lid and simmer until the liquid reduces down and a glaze starts to coat the back of a spoon. If you want a semi-burnt, richer glaze, continue stirring until the color starts to turn. Remove the pot from the heat.

3   Drain the almonds.

4   In the bowl of a Vitamix or high-speed blender, place the drained almonds, coconut oil, honey, and almond extract. Blend on medium speed, adding 1 tablespoon of coconut water at a time until you reach a consistency that is a smooth and thick cream.

5   Lift the pears out of the glaze using a slotted spoon. Arrange the pears on small dessert plates and drizzle with the glaze. Top with a dollop of almond cream.

POACHED NECTARINES

SERVES 4 A simple, elegant recipe that is delicious and light. Serve it alone or over ice cream. You can use the leftovers in Morning Polenta Porridge (page 30).

INGREDIENTI

2 cups red wine

1 cup coconut sugar

7 cups ripe medium nectarines with skins, pitted and sliced into wedges

1 teaspoon whole cloves

1 teaspoon ground cinnamon

1 teaspoon freshly squeezed lemon juice

Chamomile flowers or other edible flowers

PREPARAZIONE

1. In a medium saucepan over medium heat, place the wine and bring it to a boil. Add the coconut sugar. Stir until dissolved.

2. Add the nectarines and whole cloves. Stew for 15 minutes over medium-low heat or until the wine reduces down to form a glaze.

3. Remove the pan from the heat and stir in the cinnamon and lemon juice.

4. Transfer the mixture to a serving bowl and garnish with the edible flowers.

TAMARA'S ALMOND CAKE

SERVES 4 TO 6 I made this tasty cake for my friend's birthday picnic at the beach. It had to be vegan and gluten-free, and it had to travel well. This cake fits all those criteria, and I adore its pungent orange essence. I made it first with regular sugar but then adapted the recipe for coconut sugar. It can fall a bit in the center as it bakes, which creates a picture frame for the artful beauty of the glazed oranges.

INGREDIENTI

Coconut oil, for greasing the pan

4 medium local oranges

3 tablespoons ground flaxseeds

1½ cups coconut sugar

2 cups ground almonds

1½ teaspoons baking powder

PREPARAZIONE

1   Preheat the oven to 350 degrees F. Lightly oil
    a 9 x 9-inch pan with coconut oil and line it with
    parchment paper.

2   In a medium saucepan, place 3 of the whole
    oranges with the skins on in enough water
    to cover them. Cook them over low heat for
    2 hours. Remove the pan from the heat and
    set it aside.

3   In a small bowl, combine the flaxseeds and
    6 tablespoons of filtered water. Whisk them
    together for about 2 minutes, until the mixture
    becomes egg-like in consistency.

4   When the oranges are cool enough to handle,
    remove them from the pan, reserving the liquid.
    Cut the oranges into quarters and squeeze out
    any seeds.

5   In a large bowl fitted with an electric mixer,
    place the orange sections, 1 cup of the sugar,
    and the flaxseed mixture. Mix until well
    combined.

6   In a medium bowl, place the ground almonds and baking powder. Using a wooden spoon, combine the mixture. Gently pour the wet ingredients into the dry mixture and mix thoroughly.

7   Pour the mixture into the prepared pan and bake for 40 minutes or until a fork inserted into the center comes out clean.

8   Cut the remaining orange into thin slices revealing the floral pattern. Add the remaining ½ cup sugar to the reserved liquid and simmer the orange slices in the sugar-orange water for about 8 minutes, until the liquid reduces to a glaze.

9   When the cake has cooled, top with the glazed oranges. Serve with afternoon tea.

ALMOND MERINGUE COOKIES

MAKES EIGHT 1¹/₂-INCH COOKIES When you experience the glossy, firm peaks that dairy-free aquafaba can make, you won't be able to resist trying your hand at these irresistible cookies. May this recipe inspire you to discover a rainbow of possibilities.

INGREDIENTI

³/₄ cup aquafaba (liquid from canned garbanzo beans)

Coconut oil, for greasing the cookie sheet

1 cup superfine sugar (finely granulated white sugar) or powdered sugar

¹/₄ teaspoon cream of tartar

1 teaspoon freshly squeezed lemon juice (optional)

1 teaspoon almond extract

PREPARAZIONE

1   Preheat the oven to 350 degrees F. Grease a cookie sheet with coconut oil.

2   In a large bowl fitted with an electric mixer, whip the aquafaba on high for about 8 minutes, until it starts to get milky. Add in the sugar, cream of tartar, lemon juice, if using, and almond extract. Continue whipping for 10 minutes more, until the mixture is glossy and stiff peaks form.

3   Using a small ice-cream scoop, drop full scoops of meringue onto the prepared cookie sheet.

4   Bake for 8 minutes or until golden.

5   Cool slightly and loosen using a spatula.

EASY ALMOND ORANGE COOKIES

MAKES SIX 2-INCH COOKIES These almond butter and orange zest cookies are a twist on our Easy Peanut Butter Cookies from *The Plantpower Way*. They are not long for the cookie jar in our house. Consider making a double batch.

INGREDIENTI

3 tablespoons ground flaxseeds

1 cup almond butter

1 cup organic coconut sugar

1/2 cup garbanzo bean flour

2 teaspoons vanilla extract

1 tablespoon cacao

2 teaspoons orange zest, for garnish

Large-grain Celtic sea salt to taste

One 3.2-ounce bar of specialty dark chocolate

PREPARAZIONE

1   In a small bowl, place the flaxseeds and ¼ cup of water. Whisk until the mixture becomes sticky and egg-like. Set aside.

2   Open the almond butter and pour off any oil. If the almond butter is runny, skim off the top so you can get to the harder, thicker consistency at the bottom of the jar.

3   In a medium bowl, place the almond butter, sugar, flaxseed egg, flour, vanilla, and cacao. Use your hands to knead the dough and incorporate well. If the dough is dry and does not stick together well, add water in 2-tablespoon increments and incorporate until it sticks together.

4   Roll the dough between your hands to create small, 1½-inch balls. Place the balls 1 inch apart on an ungreased cookie sheet. Using a fork, press the balls down to flatten and mark them in either direction. Sprinkle with orange zest and salt. Place a small square of chocolate on the fork markings.

5   You can eat these cookies raw or bake them at 350 degrees F for 8 to 10 minutes. Remove them from the oven and cool. Do not overcook them or they will melt.

JUPITER GRAPE CAKE

SERVES 6 This is a traditional, simple, seasonal cake made with beautiful red Italian grapes that got their name from the Italian sanguis Jovis, "the blood of Jupiter."

INGREDIENTI

1 tablespoon coconut oil, for greasing the pan or baking sheet

1½ cups flour, plus more for dusting the pan or baking sheet

½ teaspoon Celtic sea salt

1½ cups Sangiovese grapes or any variety of red or black grape

2 teaspoons fennel seeds

2 tablespoons sugar

PREPARAZIONE

1 Preheat the oven to 350 degrees F.

2 Generously grease a 9 x 6-inch pan or rimmed baking sheet with coconut oil and dust it with flour.

3 In a large bowl, mix ½ cup water and the salt.

4 Add the flour and combine to make a dough.

5 Divide the dough in two parts. Add one to the bottom of the pan and spread evenly.

6 Add 1 cup of the grapes and sprinkle with 1 teaspoon of the fennel seeds and 1 tablespoon sugar.

7 Roll out the second part of the dough and add it on top.

8 Top with the remaining ½ cup of grapes, the remaining 1 teaspoon of fennel seeds, and the remaining 1 tablespoon of sugar.

9 Bake for 40 to 50 minutes, until the grapes are bubbling.

ACKNOWLEDGMENTS

Our deepest thanks to Lucia Watson, Anne Kosmoski, Ashley Tucker, Farin Schlussel, Nina Caldas, and the entire team at Avery/Penguin Random House for their unwavering support and beautiful design of this book.

Also to Shawn Patterson for his design contribution and overall design concept in the early stages of development.

Maclay Heriot and Leia Marasovich for their photographic genius in all aspects of this book. Your artistic captures of such precious moments and mouthwatering, delicious food are blessings to us all.

Byrd Leavell, our beloved agent at United Talent Agency, for your loyal friendship and dedicated support for our message work together and individually.

Greg, Yvonne, Julian, and Kyra Anzalone, our partners, cherished friends, and supporters in all that we create and express. Our hearts are overflowing. We love you all.

Francesco and Giovanni Toscano, founders and creators of one of the most magical places on Earth. Your dedication to excellence in every detail of Iesolana, which is permeated by your immense love of life and people. Hosting our retreats at Iesolana has been one of the great blessings of our lives.

The beautiful Iesolana family—Louise, Francesca, Camilla, Michela, Isuyinmi, Manuela, Magdalena, Andrea, Thomas, Marie, Elisa, Federica, Marianna, Aurelia, Lesyanet, and Katy. Your care and attention to create a meaningful experience has affected each of us deeply. *Grazie mille!*

Hailey Louks of the *Come Cook with Us* food blog for your contribution of pizza crust that will bless many. You rock gluten-free!

Maggie Curtis, for your attention to detail in recipe development. Thank you.

Juana Alvarenga for lovingly keeping my work space clean and organized.

Jill Zeletzki of Jillicious Journey for following your intuition and coming to serve us in the final hours of recipe testing, nutritional content, and proofing.

And to our beloved crew: Mel, Maclay, Leia, Colin, Jennifer, Angela, Tyler, Trapper, Hari, Mathis, and Jaya. You make these retreats life-changing with all that you offer. Your dedication to providing the best retreat experience on planet Earth while having fun in the process permeates the experience with the highest vibes. We love you all immensely.

RESOURCES

BOOKS

The Plantpower Way
https://www.richroll.com/the-plantpower-way/

This Cheese Is Nuts!
https://www.richroll.com/this-cheese-is-nuts/

Finding Ultra
https://www.richroll.com/shop/books/finding-ultra-signed/

Drawdown Project
http://www.drawdown.org

SUPPORT TOOLS AND ONLINE COURSES

The Plantpower Meal Planner
https://meals.richroll.com

Mindy Body Green Courses
https://www.mindbodygreen.com/classes/the-ultimate-guide-to-plant-based-nutrition

https://www.mindbodygreen.com/classes/how-to-build-a-conscious-relationship-experience-the-deepest-intimacy-of-your-l

https://www.mindbodygreen.com/wc/julie-piatt

https://www.mindbodygreen.com/wc/rich-roll

PODCASTS

The Rich Roll Podcast
http://www.richroll.com/category/podcast/

Divine Throughline Podcast
https://itunes.apple.com/us/podcast/divine-throughline/id1069738551?mt=2

FILMS

Cowspiracy
http://www.cowspiracy.com

What the Health
http://www.whatthehealthfilm.com

Kiss The Ground
https://kisstheground.com

CREW

Leia Vita Marasovich Photography
leiavitaphoto.com

Maclay Heriot Photography
https://www.maclayheriot.com

Conscious City Guide
http://www.consciouscityguide.com

Living Tea
https://www.livingtea.net

Jennifer Ayers
http://www.bloominglotusayurveda.com/contact.html

Angela Bauml Nicholas
http://www.osteopathie-praxis-ulm.de

FOOD BLOGS

Come Cook With Us
https://www.comecookwithus.co

Jilicious Journey
https://jilicious-journey.com

LOCATION

Borgo Iesolana
http://www.iesolana.it

GLOBAL TEA COMMUNITY

Global Tea Hut
https://www.globalteahut.org

CERAMICS

Roxy Faye Made Ceramics
https://www.etsy.com/shop/ROXYFAYEMADE

Plants and Magic—Jenya Melnikova
http://www.plantsandmagic.com

CONVERSION CHARTS

All conversions have been rounded up or down to the nearest whole number.

LIQUID MEASURES

US	Milliliters
1 teaspoon	5
2 teaspoons	10
1 tablespoon	14
2 tablespoons	28
1/4 cup	56
1/2 cup	120
1/3 cup	170
1 cup	240
1 1/4 cups	280
1 1/2 cups	340
2 cups	450
2 1/4 cups	500, 1/2 liter
2 1/2 cups	560
3 cups	675
3 1/2 cups	750
3 3/4 cups	840
4 cups or 1 quart	900
4 1/4 cups	1000, 1 liter
5 cups	1120

WEIGHT MEASURES

Ounces	Pounds	Grams	Kilos
1		28	
2		56	
3 1/2		100	
4	1/4	112	
5		140	
6		168	
8	1/2	225	
9		250	1/4
12	3/4	340	
16	1	450	
18		500	1/2
20	1 1/4	560	
24	1 1/2	675	
27		750	3/4
28	1 3/4	780	
32	2	900	
36	2 1/4	1000	
40	2 1/2	1100	1
48	3	1350	
54		1500	1 1/2

OVEN TEMPERATURE EQUIVALENTS

Farenheit	Celcius	Gas Mark	Description
225	110	1/4	Cool
250	130	1/2	
275	140	1	Very Slow
300	150	2	
325	170	3	Slow
350	180	4	Moderate
375	190	5	
400	200	6	Moderately Hot
425	220	7	Fairly Hot
450	230	8	Hot
475	240	9	Very Hot
500	250	10	Extremely Hot

INDEX

ABOUT THE AUTHORS

A true spiritual wellness warrior, **JULIE PIATT** (aka "SriMati") is an author, podcast host, plant-based chef, motivational speaker, meditation guide, yoga teacher, and singer. At the core of all of Julie's offerings is an opportunity for an expansion of our perspectives—a gain of cosmic view so that we all may realize our divine blueprint or life purpose.

RICH ROLL, a graduate of Stanford University and Cornell Law School, is an accomplished vegan ultra-endurance athlete, author of the #1 Amazon bestseller *Finding Ultra*, and the host of *The Rich Roll Podcast*, one of the top 100 podcasts in the world, with more than 30 million downloads since its launch in 2012. An inspiration to families worldwide he is regularly named to annual lists of the world's most influential people in health and fitness and has been featured on CNN and in the *New York Times*, the *Wall Street Journal*, *Forbes*, and *Inc.*

CONNECT WITH JULIE:

srimati.com
iTunes: Divine Throughline
🐦 📷 srimati
📘 thesrimatimusic

—

CONNECT WITH RICH:

richroll.com
iTunes: The Rich Roll Podcast
🐦 📷 richroll
📘 richrollfans

ALSO BY RICH ROLL AND JULIE PIATT

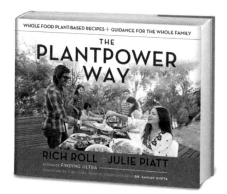

A transformative family lifestyle guide on the power of plant-based eating—with 120 recipes.

The essential primer on preparing totally vegan, nut-based cheese.

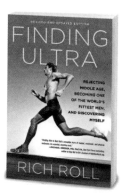

Fully revised and updated with specific dietary protocols for peak performance.